GOLDA MEIR

GOLDA

BY ELIYAHU AGRESS   • '   TRANSLATED BY ISRAEL I. TASLITT

MEIR

PORTRAIT OF A PRIME MINISTER

LAYOUT BY SHMUEL BRAND • FOREWORD BY ISRAEL GALILI

 SABRA BOOKS • NEW YORK

INTRODUCTION

BY ISRAEL GALILI

I remember Golda Meir when I was still a boy listening to the words of his mentors. Our first meeting left me with the indelible impression of a scintillating, persuasive personality endowed with the authority of leadership.

Golda Meir's innate personal authority, and her dedication to her people and its needs, prior to and following the establishment of the State of Israel, have involved her in the most decisive political and security deliberations concerning the fate of her people and Israel. In such deliberations, Golda was the only woman present, intently listening, her face marked with tension and determination and often tinged with sadness. On such occasions, when people's lives hang in the balance, there are those who will seek an easy way out by abstaining. But Golda has never shirked her responsibility — neither in political nor in military matters.

She was a steadfast participant in both debate and decision, evaluating everything in terms of morality and conscience on the one hand and political realities on the other.

Her evaluation carried special weight because of her discernment, based on rich personal and political experience over the course of many years and on numerous occasions, including the international arena.

Her speech is direct and to the point. She invests into discussion on every level, a degree of warmth, pathos and tension which nevertheless never obtrudes or prevents clear thinking. She is never indifferent. She considers that any matter referred to her merits her closest personal attention. She never uses superfluous phrases and her arguments are pertinent and convincing. Her service to her people is marked with a sense of identification and self-sacrifice. She has the courage to set out on missions by no means assured of success; the courage to express opinions without undue regard for "public relations", even if this were to bring down upon her the wrath of the press and of political adversaries.

Her behavior towards others is conditioned by her belief in the equality of all and she is never impressed by fancy titles and lofty positions. She has all her life had a tremendous respect for people who get things done, for the "toilers in the field" — the field being a kibbutz or a moshav, a port, a factory, a scientific laboratory; above all, for those called upon to serve on borders or in dangerous positions in defense of Israel's security.

Through her activities in the practical arena and in politics there runs the constant thread of participation in building and defending her country. In 1937 she was among the opponents to the Mandate's plan to partition Palestine. Her policy is based on a credo founded on the tenets of Judaism, Zionism and a love of Israel. It encompasses self-reliance, a rejection of any trend which may erode Judaism, extreme caution against illusions and pious utterances of dubious worth, and faith in deeds and not merely words.

Golda rose to her position in the leadership of the nation by way of service to the Zionist Movement abroad, pioneering work in Eretz Yisrael, service to the Labor Movement, numerous important missions and appointments in several cabinets, as Minister of Labor and Foreign Minister.

She set the highest standards in all these — in the field of labor legislation and industrial endeavor; missions to the Jewish people; as the first Ambassador to the U.S.S.R.; and in establishing relations between Israel and newly developing nations in far-off countries.

Eventually, in the fateful course of events, she has been called upon to head the Government of the State of Israel. Although she never reached out to such an exalted position, and although it has virtually been thrust on her, she has accepted the greatest responsibility in her career, and has proved magnificently that she is worthy of the honor.

Jerusalem,
December, 1969.

Minister of Information
ISRAEL GALILI

We all come from an area which is a very ancient one. The hills and the valleys of the region have been witnesses to many wars and many conflicts. But that is not the only thing which characterizes that part of the world from which we come. It is also a part of the world which has given to humanity three great religions. It is also that part of the world which has given a code of ethics to all humanity. In our countries, in the entire region, all our peoples are anxious for and in need of a higher standard of living, of great programmes of development and progress.

Can we, from now on—all of us—turn a new leaf and, instead of fighting with each other, can we all, united, fight poverty and disease and illiteracy? Is it possible for us to put all our efforts and all our energy into one single purpose, the betterment and progress and development of all our lands and all our peoples?

I can here pledge the Government and the people of Israel to do their part in this united effort. There is no limit to what we are prepared to contribute so that all of us, together, can live to see a day of happiness for our peoples and see again from that region a great contribution to peace and happiness for all humanity.

From Foreign Minister Golda Meir's Speech
at the General Assembly, 11th Session of the United Nations,
March 1, 1957

THE
EARLY
YEARS

"I, Golda Meir, pledge allegiance, as Prime Minister, to the State of Israel and its laws, to fulfill my post of Prime Minister in good faith and to carry out the resolutions of the Knesset..."

The pledge of allegiance was enunciated with quiet confidence, tinged by a note of emotion and trepidation. Golda Meir, member of the Knesset, stepped down from the rostrum and took her seat at the Cabinet table, in the Prime Minister's chair. The fourteenth Israel Government was now headed by a woman — the first member of her sex to serve as Israel's Prime Minister, and the third woman in the world, counting India's Indira Ghandi and Ceylon's Mrs. Bandaranaike, to be a head of State.

Golda Meir proceeded to introduce her Cabinet and to deliver her inaugural address before the Knesset at that historic session on March 17, 1969 — a brief, bold, dynamic speech, devoid of fanciful phraseology. It was a typical presentation that personified her character : clear, direct, without sophistry, double meanings or verbal acrobatics.

The reactions to her address lasted five hours. Golda Meir, Premier of Israel, sat quietly, listening to the words of praise heaped upon her by spokesmen for the various political parties represented in the legislature. Even Rabbi Isaac Meir Lewin, head of Agudat Israel, who voted against the new Government on the grounds that *halachic* (religious) law prohibits the leadership of a Jewish Government by a member of the female sex, lauded Mrs. Meir's distinguished record of service to the nation.

During those five hours of speech-making there passed before her mind's eye the long road she had traveled and the milestones on the way : Kiev, Pinsk, Milwaukee, the settlement Merhaviah, Tel Aviv, Jerusalem, Moscow, the capitals of

Golda as a young child, the first photograph of Israel's future Premier, taken in Pinsk, Ukraine, Russia. The pleated skirt, hair ribbon and flower were typical props of the time.

Asian and African countries that had gained independence in recent times... truly an amazing life story, filled with ceaseless and untiring work, in missions and posts of all kinds.

The story, which began 71 years ago in Kiev, capital of the Ukraine, unfolds in logical sequence — childhood years in Pinsk and the Russian bogs, early maturity in Milwaukee (where she first entered public life), followed by five decades of dynamic, fruitful activity in what was to become the State of Israel. In Palestine-Israel, her work took her from rural Merhaviah to the Women's Working Council, to the Histadrut executive, to Brenner House in Tel Aviv, to vital political missions on behalf of the Jewish Agency prior to the establishment of Israel. After Israel's independence was proclaimed, she served as Ambassador to the Soviet Union, as Minister of Labor, as Foreign Minister, as Secretary of the dominant Mapai party — and now the heaviest burden of all had been placed on her shoulders, as Prime Minister.

Golda Meir was one of eight children born to Moshe Yitzhak and Bluma (Neiditch) Mabowehz. She was born on May 3, 1898, in Kiev. Her father, a cabinetmaker, worked hard to provide a living, however meager, for his family of four boys and four girls. The boys died as infants and only three daughters survived : Sheine, the eldest, Golda, and Zippora, now living in the United States.

Golda's childhood was not a happy one; it left two indelible impressions on her : the dread of pogroms and the fear of hunger. She recalls :

"There was a rumor of a pogrom brewing in Kiev. Papa reacted to it as I had known him to react all his life — he made no arrangements to

Golda Meir's grandparents in the Ukraine, Russia.

hide the family, but tried instead to bolster the doorway by clapping boards on to the door. Fortunately the pogrom did not materialize." To this she adds: "If a person can, in his lifetime, move on from defense against hooligans in Kiev to the opportunity of living in the State of Israel, where he is not an outcast, where he can protect his children — what more can one ask of Israel?"

"I well remember the hunger. One scene has remained with me: our little sister was then an infant, hardly more than six months old. Mama made porridge, a great luxury in those days. Mama gave some to me and the rest she gave to my little sister. She finished hers before I did, and Mama took some of mine. I remember how shocked I was because something I had been given — a rare occurance — had been taken away from me."

She recalled this searing experience of once being a hungry child when a newspaper correspondent asked her about the prospects of peace between Israel and the Arab states. "This will come about," she replied, "when Nasser, and all the other Arab leaders will understand that peace is as vital for their peoples as it is for us. This isn't a gift that he can bestow on us. This is something that his children, the children in the Nile Valley, need as much as we do ... This will come about when Nasser awakens one morning after a sleepless night, worried — not because he is not clever enough to figure out a detailed plan for killing Israelis, but because of his people — impoverished, ignorant, blighted with a high rate of infant mortality in Egypt ... when saving the lives of his children will mean more to him than killing Israelis."

Little Golda was five years old when the family moved to Pinsk, the home of her mother's family. Her father, like so many others in those days, took to "the fortune trail" — America.

Moshe Yitzhak, like so many of his contemporaries on the trail of quick wealth, lived at first in New York. He found work that paid him three dollars a week, part of which he sent home.

From New York he moved on to Milwaukee, where a better paying job had been promised him.

In Pinsk, the eldest daughter, Sheine, then in her middle teens, had joined the illegal Zionist-Socialist revolutionary movement. Seven-year-old Golda used to hide behind the hearth in the house and listen to her sister and her fellow revolutionaries plot the fall of the Czarist regime and plan the rise of a new society.

Golda Meir recalls those anxious times when Sheine would disappear from the house early in the evening and not return until late at night.

"We were living then not far from the police station, and could hear the horrible cries of young men and women arrested for their illegal activities and beaten mercilessly. Those were days when the Cossacks were brought into Pinsk.

"Galloping astride their horses, they trampled people in their way and whipped every young person they could find. That was when Mama

began writing to Papa, that because of my sister's activities, it would be impossible for us to remain in Pinsk. We had to leave for America."

The family left Russia in 1906 and journeyed to Milwaukee, where the father was now working in the city's railroad yard; he was also a member of the labor movement and of his trade union. The mother, an extremely energetic woman, augmented the family income by operating a dairy store. Young Golda helped her mother, after school hours. She dreamt of becoming a teacher, but her parents did little to encourage her.

Sheine recalls that period well:

"In the United States, the school year begins early in September. During the few months before school opened, Golda had already managed to master the rudiments of the English language so that by the time she entered school she could understand what was being spoken all around her. It didn't take her long to adapt herself to the study program and school life.

A Shavuot picnic attended by her fellow Milwaukee young Zionists found Golda sporting a traditional floral wreath in her hair. (For a better view, see the enlargement.)

Elementary school graduation was a time for photographs. Golda, seated second from left in front row, was one of the youngest in the class.

"Golda showed signs of unusual talent from the very beginning. She excelled in all her school subjects, as well as in English. But at home she had to bear the burdens, because of me. My Socialist principles forbade my helping Mama in the 'capitalist' store. When I quarreled with my parents and left home, Golda had to spend many hours behind the counter, and she was still a child. She used to open the store early in the morning and stay until Mama returned from the wholesale market with fruits and vegetables for the day's business. More than once this made Golda late for school; every time she came late she was very upset, and when she came home there was much crying and shouting, but it did her no good. The livelihood of the family was at stake.

"Golda's tardiness and absences didn't go unnoticed in class. One day a truant officer came to the house and told my parents, in no uncertain terms, that the law required every child under 14 to attend school regularly. The warning made it more difficult for Mama; she now arose earlier to go to market, but Golda would still be late for school occasionally.

"Golda's strong will and good mind overcame the obstacles in her way — it was a knack she had had from early childhood. In school she continued doing well, and she was much liked and respected both by her classmates and her teachers. She had her troubles and her compensations.

"Golda's interest in public service was evident even when she was still in school. Her first concern was for her classmates who where too poor to buy school books. She approached the wealthier girls, and sometimes their mothers. She organized a gathering, her very first one, with public announcements, in a rented hall on a Saturday night. The other girls and their mothers came, as did important people from the neighborhood. Golda was the chairman. She explained the reason for the gathering and how important it was to have mutual help operate inside the school. Word of the gathering got around, and Golda, who was all of 12 at the time, received more praise. More

important, many pockets and pocketbooks came open that evening, and a fund to help needy pupils was organized on the spot. Papa and Mama were bursting with pride."

Sheine went to live in Denver, where she married Shamai Korngold and raised a family. Golda, now 14, ran away from home to her sister and enrolled in a Denver high school; a year and a half later her parents became reconciled with her ardent desire to keep on studying, and she returned to Milwaukee. From high school she went on to a teachers' college.

"Our home," relates Golda Meir, "was in keeping with Jewish tradition. Papa sent me and my little sister to a Talmud Torah, since there was no other Hebrew school. We didn't come away with a very impressive stock of Hebrew. On the other hand, we did very well with Yiddish, the language spoken at home. We had a daily Yiddish newspaper and many Yiddish books in the house. Itinerant Yiddish lecturers never went to a hotel in Milwaukee for lodgings; we had a sofa in our home, and the intellectuals who slept on it gave it a sort of fame and honor. The house was always alive with public affairs; our family never limited itself to matters of personal interest.

"Mama used to help other families. Both she and Papa were members of B'nai B'rith, and Mama was particularly active. All sorts of benefits were held to raise money for the poor families. There were also the new immigrants who came to the city, in that large wave of immigration prior to the first World War. Papa was active in a society for overseas aid and, later, in the American Jewish Congress."

Golda worked along with her father, during the first World War, in an organization called "Aid in Need," established by Jewish workers in Milwaukee to help European Jews caught in the maelstrom of war and violence. She also belonged

At eighteen, Golda was graduated from teachers college. The year was 1916 — and a remarkable career lay ahead.

LOUISE G. BORN

Classical Course; Girls' Club; Lincoln; Pageant.

*"Ready to make a day of night,
Goddess excellently bright!"*

Louise Born.

HARRY MARTENS

Science Course; President M. N. D.; Football, '12, '14, '15; Senior Play; Track, '12, '13; Basket Ball, '12, '13, '14; Cap't. Indoor Baseball, '15.

"Has a smile for everybody."

Harry Martens

GOLDIE MABOWEHZ

Elective Course, 3 yrs.; Lincoln Society; Science Club; Pageant.

*"Those about her
From her shall read the perfect ways
of honor."*

Goldie Mabowehz

WILLIAM L. KICKHAEFER

Science Course; Lincoln; Gridiron; Senior Vaudeville, '15; Pageant.

*"Frequently seen in public places,
Social dances, sports and races."*

PEARL GILBERT

Commercial Course, 3½ yrs.; Palladium; Girls' Club.

*"The learning ear is always found
close to the speaking tongue."*

13

On December 24, 1917, Golda was married to Morris Meyerson.

The vision of young Golda, as seen by the Philadelphia photographer, Darry. ▷

Golda was very close to her sister Sheina and her family, and often visited Sheina and her husband and growing family in Denver.

16

to a literary club, where she attended lectures and discussions.

Here Golda showed herself to be a gifted speaker; even her father was impressed by her public speaking. She recalls:

"In those days it was customary to hold speeches in the open air, since this saved the cost of renting a hall.

"One evening, as I was about to leave the house, Papa asked: Where to?' I told him I had to make a speech on a street corner. Papa was outraged: 'What? A Mabowehz daughter in the street? You're not going!' I told him that my friends were waiting for me, but he was not to be moved. "You won't go!' he repeated. But I went — even though he threatened to drag me off the stand by my hair.

"I came to the street corner. My friends were in high spirits. I told them: 'I want you to know that we're going to have a scandal here.' I was the second or third speaker. I said my piece, and I was plenty scared — but nothing happened. I came home late. Mama was up and waiting. I asked her: 'Where's Papa?' Mama said that he was asleep, then added: 'He came into the house and said: I didn't know that she had it in her.' I had impressed Papa so much that he forgot to drag me off by my hair. I've always considered that speech the finest I ever made in my life!"

Golda's first job, after graduation, was teaching in a Yiddish-speaking *Folks Shule*, which was steeped in Labor Zionism. It was then that she joined the Poale Zion (Labor Zionist) party, but, she says, "not before I had decided to go to the Land of Israel. I suppose my grasp of Zionism was quite fundamental; I couldn't understand how one could be a Zionist without going there. In 1917, Ben Zvi, Ben Gurion and Zerubavel, then under banishment from Palestine by the Turkish authorities, visited Milwaukee, which was known as a warm Zionist city with a devoted branch of the party. When I joined it there was no doubt about my *aliyah*, (immigration) at the very first opportunity.

"When I left America I was fully aware of the meaning of its freedom, its opportunities, its beautiful countryside. I loved America, but once I reached the Land of Israel I didn't experience a single moment of longing; it felt so natural for me to be there."

Golda's *aliyah* took place four years after her marriage to Morris Meyerson, whom she had met in her sister's home in Denver.

Golda's decision to make her *aliyah* came when she was 17, one year after she first met Morris. He was not a Zionist. His socialism was cosmopolitan.

On a mission to America for Palestine, in 1929 Golda posed with a girl friend in New York.

The year was 1921, and the dream of settling in Palestine and building a Jewish Homeland would soon be realized. The Meyersons — Golda, second row, extreme left, and her husband, top row, second from left — are shown with young Zionist pioneers at a gathering in Franklin Park in Boston before departing from America. The trip to the Promised Land took 54 days.

Golda told Morris that their marriage would come about only if he agreed to go to Palestine and to live in a *kvutzah* (an agricultural colony). After some tribulation, Morris yielded; they were married on December 24, 1917.

Golda gave up teaching and devoted herself to party activities, until the couple was able to save enough money for the trip. On May 19, 1921, together with Sheine and her two children, they sailed for the Promised Land on the "Pocahontas." The voyage took 54 days and was filled with adventures, danger and agitation. The ship was a shoddy vessel; fire broke out on board as she put out to sea, the crew mutinied several times, the engines broke down repeatedly, the chief engineer was murdered. The "Pocahontas" had to put in at Alexandria instead of Jaffa; because of the 1921 Arab rioting, the Arab owners of rowboats in Jaffa harbor refused to transfer Jewish passengers from the ship to shore. The five passengers reached Tel Aviv on July 14, by train from Alexandria.

FROM
MERHAVIAH
TO
INDEPENDENCE

"We decided to go to a *kvutzah*," relates Golda, "while we were still in America. I had a friend in Merhaviah — Dubinsky, who came with the Jewish Legion. Volunteers for the Legion left from our home, each with a small bag that Mama sewed and filled with goodies. But we had to wait. In those days, new members were taken into the *kvutzah* around *Rosh Hashanah,* when everyone had to declare whether he was remaining or not, and thus it was not known how many openings there were. We made our application to Merhaviah, and it was voted on at three different meetings. They had nothing against Morris but I was an American girl, and what American girl would agree to live and labor in a *kvutzah?* At the third meeting they finally decided to take us in. I still believe that the scales were tipped in our favor by the phonograph we had brought along ! It was the first phonograph in the country without the horn — and many records came with it. It's still there in Merhaviah !

"My sister, her two children and a few others occupied one dwelling in Tel Aviv, as we waited for Merhaviah to open its gates to us. An apartment, at that time, could be rented for five pounds monthly, payable one year in advance. This was too expensive for us. We finally found two rooms in Nveh Zedek, on Lillienblum Street — the kitchen and utilities were outside. The phonograph drew avid listeners to our home every evening.

"A few months later we went to the *kvutzah,* while my sister and her two children remained in Tel Aviv."

In Merhaviah, Golda was one of eight women among 32 men. From her very first day there, she fought for equal working rights with the men. "In Merhaviah, I won my first battle in the country," she recalls. "We had a large water tower, the top of which could be reached by climbing a steep, narrow iron ladder. In those days we

Later in the year 1921, Golda was already working in the settlement of Merhaviah. Her duties included harvesting the crops.

At a Zionist convention held in the United States, Golda is shown with (to her left) Zalman Shazar, today the President of Israel, and in front row, left, David Ben Gurion, and right, Yitzhak Ben Zvi, second President of Israel.

often had breaks in the kitchen water supply and the girls had to wait until the caretaker got around to climbing the narrow ladder. One day I was on kitchen duty when the water stopped flowing. I climbed up the ladder and turned on the valve. As I returned to the kitchen, from the looks of amazement on everyone's face, I sensed that I had entered a new phase. I had in fact overcome the 'American' block in my *aliyah*."

Though Golda worked everywhere in the *kvutzah*, her main responsibility was the chicken coop, which gave her great satisfaction until one night

when a fox broke into the coops and wreaked havoc — the sight of the massacre that greeted Golda in the morning remained with her for a long time.

Soon Golda's talents in administration came to notice. She was appointed to represent the *kvutzah* in the Histadrut council. Golda asked for permission to address the group in Yiddish; only Hebrew was permitted for anyone who had been in the country more than two years. She preferred Yiddish because she felt that she could express her thoughts much better in that language. The

Golda was in no time at all involved in work for the budding Labor Party. Here she is seen adressing delegates at a Party convention.

permission given her to do so signified the high regard that the council had for her opinion.

For Golda, the two years that she and her husband lived with the *kvutzah* were filled with happiness. But *kvutzah* life was not for Morris Meyerson. He did not manage to become part of the colony, and the physical labor was too much for him. His letters to his mother in America were full of gloomy reflections on his life in Palestine. Mrs. Meyerson senior pleaded with the couple to return to the United States, but Golda would not hear of it. The young couple reached a compromise — to leave the *kvutzah* but to remain in the country.

The two left Merhaviah in 1923 and moved to Tel Aviv. Golda became a cashier in the Histadrut's public works office and worked there until the birth of her son, Menahem, in 1924. The family then moved to Jerusalem and Morris found employment as a bookkeeper. Their daughter, Sarah, was born in Jerusalem in 1926.

Those four years, between 1924 and 1928, in Jerusalem, Golda recalls, were the most burdensome in her life. The family lived in want. Golda was tied down to the house and to her family, far removed from any public activity. She felt she simply could not go on with this type of life for very long. Her friends soon learned that she was yearning to return to public life, and her party, *Ahdut Avoda,* found a position for her as secretary of the Histadrut's *Moetzet Hapoalot* (the Working Women's Council). The gate to her activities on a national scale had swung open. This was to be her one and only post with a women's organization. From there she went on to general public offices, in the Histadrut, the Jewish Agency and the Government of Israel. In all her years of public service she never regarded herself as set apart from her male colleagues; she asked for no special favors and never considered herself at a disadvantage because of her sex.

These were also the years when she represented the Working Women's Council on international commissions. In 1932 she was sent to the United States for a two-year period to represent the Council with its sister organization there, the Pioneer Women.

Returning to Palestine in 1934, she went to work with the Histadrut's executive committee, the top body of the country's laborers, occupying posts of growing importance, first as director of the committee's tourist department, then as a member of the committee's secretariat — a very high rung on the ladder. For several years she headed the mutual aid department, then she was put in charge of the Histadrut's pension invest-

During World War II, Golda visited units of the Jewish Brigade.

Golda goes on an overseas mission.

Family time during a visit to the United States.

Delegates at the 1946 World Zionist Congress.

Listening attentively to speakers at the 1946 Zionist Congress, where an assessment of the Jewish people's losses during World War II produced a mood of shock — and determination.

Golda, as a private person, free from public issues.

Golda, in 1930 on a mission to the United States.

ment institutions and later served as chairman of the national supervisory commission of Kupat Holim, the Sick Fund. She was also in charge of the Trade Union and Labor Relations Council.

Early in these days of Golda's public service, her party merged with Hapoel Hatzair (The Young Laborer) and Golda became one of the prime movers in the new party. She supported David Ben Gurion when the latter signed an agreement with Ze'ev Jabotinsky in 1934, which did away with the antagonism between left and right-wing labor (Ben Gurion's opponents excoriated the limitation on strikes and the compulsory arbitration which the agreement stipulat-

ed). On another occasion, in 1937, when the leadership was split over the Palestine Partition Plan of the Peel Commission, Golda differed with Ben Gurion, who supported the Plan. Her reasoning was that partition was unacceptable because its implementation would not guarantee an end to the disturbances, and there was no assurance that the Jewish community would ever be strong enough to change the set boundaries, since in her opinion only wars could change boundaries.

The scope of Golda's activities in the Histadrut, the National Council and the Zionist movement left her with little time for her home life. In the early forties the Meyersons separated, the children

As chairman of the Agency's political department.

As general secretary of the Labor Party.

remaining with their mother. Both Menahem and Sarah studied music ; Menahem became a cellist, but Sarah's violin lessons were cut short because of the expense. They often accompanied their mother on visits to friends — people like Zalman Shazar, today Israel's President, and Ziama Aranne, among many others.

Golda's children learned from her the importance of being associated with worthwhile causes. They also acquired the trait of humility. "It wasn't proper to boast of Mama's position," says Sarah. "When I had to fill out questionnaires and state the occupation of my parents, I always got around it by saying that my mother was working for the Histadrut."

Golda's parents came to Palestine in 1926 and settled in Herzliyah. The entire family was now together, except for Zippora. Golda recalls, with nostalgia : "The two families used to gather in the home of our parents on holidays, especially on Passover and Rosh Hashanah. My sister's children and my own still remember with great pleasure those wonderful days with their grandparents — their grandmother's holiday fish and *strudel* and grandfather's melodies, which they still hum.

"Papa used to stand watch in the settlement. He got to know the Haganah and the Histadrut.

Leaders of the Jewish community in Mandated Palestine launched a hunger strike in sympathy with a boatload of postwar Jewish refugees who had been denied entry. The scene is outside the Jewish public buildings in Jerusalem; the year, 1946.

He was very friendly with Shprinzak (Joseph Shprinzak, Israel's first Speaker of the Knesset). The house in Herzliyah became a center for the needy. That's how Papa lived all his life. He died at the age of 79, and until the last six months, when he was ill, he was tall, straight and handsome."

At the outbreak of the second World War, the Jewish community in Palestine consisting of 600,000 souls was faced with a double challenge, as Ben Gurion put it: to fight Britain's White Paper restricting Jewish immigration as if there were no Hitler and to fight Hitler, the common enemy, as if there were no White Paper. Golda was active on both fronts, cooperating with the Mandatory Government in the joint war effort of marshaling resources and recruiting soldiers, and battling the same regime to prevent the implementation of the White Paper.

Golda undertook to head the political section of the Histadrut at the end of 1940, after Dov Hoz, the section's coordinator, was killed in a traffic accident.

In this capacity, Golda appeared as a witness in the famous Haganah trial of 1943. Speaking in the name of the Histadrut executive, she gave impressive testimony at the trial of two Haganah members, Avraham Reichlin and Aryeh Sirkin (now Aryeh Sarig, Deputy Director-General of the Defense Ministry), who were brought up before the British military tribunal in Jerusalem on charges of acquiring arms for the Haganah from a batch of arms stolen from the military arsenal. Her appearance, on September 7, 1943, as witness for the defense was a source of national pride.

"Her words," the press reported, "were listened to with rapt attention. She replied with forthrightness and spirit." At the conclusion of her testimony, the president judge of the tribunal remarked that "this testimony is sufficiently clear."

Golda's words were clear indeed. Commenting on the right of the Jews to self-defense, she declared: "If the Jew who bears arms in his own defense is guilty, then all the Jews in the Land of Israel are guilty. If a Jew or Jewess who uses weapons for self-protection is a criminal you will have to build many new prisons."

Golda replied to the prosecutor's interrogation about the Haganah and the Palmach directly and without evasion. She described the riots and the disturbances that had been perpetrated in Palestine against Jewish settlement. "Everyone in this country, including the British authorities," she said, "knows that without the defense put up by the Jewish community, little would have remained of either life or property."

The testimony brought on some heated exchanges of words between Golda and the prosecutor and the presiding judge, but she came through with flying colors.

The second World War ended with victory of the Allies, and the Jewish community in Palestine plunged into its own struggle against the British Mandatory Government, demanding that the gates of the country be opened to the Jews who had survived the European holocaust.

The British, for their part, practically declared war on the "illegal immigration" movement, and sent warships to trail blockade-running vessels carrying thousands of refugees from their points of embarkation. In the Italian port of La Spezia, the hundreds of immigrants who were aboard the "Feda," which had been prevented by British pressure from sailing, declared a hunger strike. They announced that they would keep the strike going until they received permission to sail for Palestine.

The Jewish community in Palestine was up in arms. At a session of the National Council which considered ways and means of dealing with the situation, Golda proposed that the heads of the community proclaim a fast in solidarity with those aboard the blockade-runner, and that the fast should last as long as the immigrants would continue with it, and — if the Jewish refugees were not permitted entry — the fasting should continue to its bitter end.

The National Council, along with the Jewish

Golda, accompanied by David Remez, chairman of the National Council photographed in Jerusalem.

Agency executive, approved the proposal. Three days before Passover in 1946, the leaders of the Jewish community began their fast.

The hunger strike endured for 101 hours and ended only after the British High Commissioner promised that the 'Feda" would be released and the 1,200 blockade-runners would be allowed entry.

Golda and her fellow hunger strikers never forgot the Passover Seder held that year. Conducted in the courtyard of the national buildings in Jerusalem, the Seder participants sat until midnight, reciting the traditional *Haggadah* story of the Israelites' exodus from Egypt, and thinking of the exodus of Jews from postwar Europe. After the fasting and the Seder were over, Golda was taken to the hospital for brief treatment.

On June 29, 1946 — the notorious "Black Sabbath" — the British authorities suddenly swooped down and arrested all the Jewish leaders who were in Palestine at the time. When Moshe

Shertok (later Sharett, who served as Foreign Minister and for a short time as Prime Minister) was detained and imprisoned in the Latrun camp, Mrs. Meyerson was given responsibility for his post as political director of the Jewish Agency.

In the course of the struggle, the British soldiers conducted an unrelenting search for hidden arms. Their action at the time was notorious for its brutality. As acting head of the political division of the Jewish Agency, Golda minced no words in condemning these acts by the British.

On September 1, 1946, addressing a press conference following an exceptionally brutal search by the British for arms in Ruhamah and Dorot, she said : "Removal of these arms actually means

At a meeting of Palestine's Jewish leaders in 1947.

With Remez and Dr. Nahum Goldmann.

With Eliezer Kaplan, Israel's first Minister of Finance, left, and Reuven Shiloah, at a U.N. commission session in 1947.

At a reception for James G. McDonald, who was visiting Palestine on a fact-finding tour for the United Nations.

The twenty-fifth anniversary of Jewish settlement of the Jezreel Valley region was celebrated in the Ein Harod kibbutz. Golda is shown at the main table.

an invitation to destroy Ruhamah for the third time (the settlement had been evacuated and destroyed in the violent periods of 1929 and 1936). We cannot yield these arms, since past experience has taught us that we cannot place our trust in anyone who will guarantee our safety in time of need — except in our own selves."

In the leadership debates over the struggle

against the British, Golda was among the "hawks," advocating a total campaign. Soon after the "Black Sabbath," Golda told the Histadrut council: "I am sure that there are ways and means to bring the community to a civil rebellion and disobedience in many aspects of our lives. I am aware of the difficulties. I know that once we embark on this course, it will be as none of its forerunners; it cannot and should not be similar. After all, something did happen in this land."

These utterances voiced Golda's deep concern and sense of responsibility for the future of the community and of the Jewish people, but they also reflected her conviction that there was no alternative; she believed fully that inaction would bring on disaster.

On one occasion Golda met with the secretary of the Mandatory regime, Ernie Garney, to discuss the matter of transferring to Palestine a few immigrants who had been deported to Cyprus. As was her custom, Golda spoke with deep emotion about the suffering of the survivors of the Nazi holocaust. Garney blandly suggested that Hitler wouldn't have persecuted the Jews to such a degree if his charges wouldn't have had some substance of truth. Golda didn't try to argue with him. She arose, looked at Garney and said: "That's what all the anti-Semites say," and slammed the door. She refused to meet with him ever again.

This particular period recorded several meetings which Golda had with the heads of the British Mandatory Government. From the British viewpoint, the strong stand that she took was tantamount to arrogance; she behaved at the time as though she were the representative of a sovereign Government.

After the end of the second World War, Golda concentrated her efforts within Palestine and in the world Jewish community, as well as on the international arena, on behalf of the immediate establishment of a Jewish state. At the 22nd Zionist Congress, convened late in 1946, she said:

"When did the idea of the state come up — not as a distant, ultimate goal — but as something indispensable? It came up when we Jews in the Land of Israel, six hundred thousand strong, despite everything we had achieved and with all that we had undergone during the long war years, found ourselves helpless in the face of the need to rescue hundreds and thousands, perhaps millions of Jews from certain death, when the sole

barrier between us and them, between our will and readiness to save them and the horrible certainty that they were doomed to annihilation at Hitler's hands, was the policy, the regime and the regulation set for us by foreigners — the White Paper!

"It was then that we realized the imperative need for the state, not as the ultimate goal but as the only feasible way for rescuing Jews and building the Land of Israel — the imperative need to have the project and the tools in our hands."

In 1947 Golda carried on negotiations with the British authorities for the release of families with children from the detention camps of Cyprus. The British agreed, on condition that their number would be included in the monthly quota of immigrants released and allowed entry. It was necessary to persuade the thousands of childless immigrants to give up their turn and wait months — perhaps years — for their release.

Golda volunteered to carry out the thankless task. She spoke to scores of immigrant groups, and her eloquence and sincerity persuaded them to accept an arrangement which would discriminate against them but would make it possible to remove the children from the detention camps.

During the stormy period between November 1947 and May 1948 — the violent months preceding the War of Independence and Israel's birth, when the Arab armies invaded the country from the south, east and north and bands of marauders roamed the countryside — Golda carried out several secret political missions and twice went to talk to American Jewry. "When the history of this period will be written," David Ben Gurion said later, "it will tell about a Jewish woman who obtained the funds to assure the existence of the State in its first days."

Many stories have been recounted of Golda's two meetings with King Abdullah, the ruler of Jordan, in November of 1947, just before the adoption of the United Nations resolution calling for the establishment of a Jewish State in a part of Palestine, and on May 10, 1948, four days

before the proclamation of the State and the attack on Israel by the Arab armies.

The first meeting took place in the home of Pinhas Rutenberg, near the Aram-Naharayim power station. Golda went to that meeting with Eliyahu Sasson and Ezra Danin, then the heads of the Arab division of the Jewish Agency. The meeting was arranged after intimation had been received that Abdullah was prepared to talk the situation over with the representatives of the Jewish community. He was eager to study the possibility of preventing an Arab-Jewish war, into which he would be drawn, against his own interests, particularly since the establishment of an Arab state in a part of Palestine would be headed by his sworn enemy, Haj Amin al-Husseini, the Grand Mufti of Jerusalem. Golda went to the meeting to persuade Abdullah not to join the other Arab states in their invasion plans.

King Abdullah was amazed to find a woman at the head of the Jewish delegation, but he was reassured when it was explained to him that she was only filling in for Moshe Shertok. Abdullah proposed the establishment of "an independent republic in part of Palestine, with a Transjordan state which would take in both sides of the Jordan River which he would rule, and whose economy, armed forces and legislatures would be shared jointly."

The members of the delegation pointed out that the Palestine issue was being taken up by the United Nations, and that they were hopeful of a decision to set up two states, Jewish and Arab, and that they wished to discuss with him an agreement based on this decision.

Abdullah agreed and proposed that another meeting be held after November 29th, "at which time we shall discuss ways of co-operation in the light of the resolution." He also wanted to know

One of the late General Orde Wingate's great admirers, Golda is shown in 1947 speaking at a ceremony marking the dedication of the Wingate Forest.

how the Jews would react to an attempt on his part to annex the "Arab portion" of Palestine. "I want to add this portion to my kingdom, and I do not want a new Arab state, which would interfere with my plans and enable the other Arabs to boss me."

The Jewish representatives replied in the affirmative, 'provided that this would not interfere with the founding of our state and provided that this would not lead to a clash with your forces, and provided that this action would be taken along with a declaration that the annexation is intended only to institute order and assure peace until the United Nations would be able to set up a government in that portion."

Months passed. Word was received that Abdullah intended breaking his promise and that his Arab Legion would join the Arab forces in an attempt to destroy Israel as soon as it was proclaimed. In April of 1948, Golda got a secret message through to Abdullah, asking him if he was going to keep the promise he had made at their meeting. The King replied : "I am a Bedouin, and a word of honor is sacred to us ; secondly, I am the King, and my word obligates my government ; thirdly, I never break any word I have given to a woman."

Evidently the pressures on Abdullah were proving to be stronger than his promise to Golda. The heads of the Jewish Agency decided to make another attempt to come to an understanding with Abdullah. Again fate willed it that Golda should go, this time to Amman, at the King's request.

Golda was then living in beleaguered Jerusalem. She arrived in Tel Aviv in a tiny, single-engine plane for a meeting with Ben Gurion, and from there she went on with Ezra Danin to Haifa, where she obtained traditional Arab dress and set out for Naharayim, changing cars along the route to throw off any possible pursuit. In Naharayim, Golda donned her Arab clothes and left with Danin (also disguised as an Arab) for Amman ; the trip was made in the darkness of the night, in a special car sent by the King. The

At meetings and gatherings in all parts of the United States, immediately after the proclamation of Israel statehood, Golda won the hearts of men and women everywhere.

mission was top secret even as far as the Arab left no doubt that he was more concerned about his British patrons than his fear of the Arab rulers. Abdullah made a final attempt to avoid a war : the Jews would not proclaim their sovereignty and would halt immigration, at least for a few months. He proposed that all of western Palestine be made part of his kingdom and promised that the Jews would have full representation in the Jordan parliament.

Abdullah, always an admirer of the agriculture and other developments achieved by the Jewish community, expressed sorrow over the impending sentries were concerned ; tension had mounted to such a pitch that revelation of the passengers' identities at any one of the check-points would have endangered their lives.

Golda and Danin passed the ten check-points to Amman without incident. The Jordanian chauffeur drove them immediately to the home of a wealthy Arab of Amman, a confidant of the King.

The King arrived a short while later, in a black mood. The conversation lasted about an hour. The King did not try to deny the promise he had made in November, but he argued that the situation had changed drastically in the meantime.

"Then I was free to make decisions. Now I am only one of five," the King said. His intimations destruction. He begged Golda to agree to his proposal. "I don't understand," said the King, "why the Jews are in such a hurry."

Golda replied, with characteristic directness, that two thousand years of waiting didn't sound to her like haste ; she rejected the proposal on the spot. 'If your statement is intended to mean that a Jewish state should not be proclaimed, and that if it is, war will follow, then let there be war.

"Perhaps," she added, "we shall yet meet again — after the founding of the Jewish state." The King despaired of the argument and turned, in a fatherly way, to Ezra Danin, imploring him, as one born in the East, to make Golda change her mind.

Flanked by Henry Morgenthau Jr. and Sen. Herbert H. Lehman, during her 1948 campaign to raise funds for the infant State.

The meeting ended fruitlessly. However, toward the end of the War of Independence when Abdullah met Moshe Dayan, the King of Jordan cast the entire blame for the war on Golda. "Had it not been for her stubbornness," he said, "all this fighting could have been prevented."

After this meeting, Golda Meir reported that "my impression of the talk was that Abdullah isn't going into battle with gladness and self-assurance. Actually he doesn't want it; he is afraid of defeat and even more afraid of his partners, both the Arab states and the British. However he has gotten himself entangled in the mesh set for him by the British and now he can't get out of it."

The mission failed. Golda rushed back to Tel Aviv in order to participate in the ceremonies marking the proclamation of the State of Israel. She was one of the signatories of Israel's Declaration of Independence.

Prior to this historic event, in January of 1948,

Golda went on an important mission to the United States. Palestinian Jewry was confronted with grave risks because of the lack of arms. It became increasingly clear that the Jewish defense forces would require artillery, tanks and planes. The sums needed to acquire this material were, in terms of those days, astronomical. Men were sent to Europe to purchase arms virtually empty-handed. The Jewish Agency treasurer, Eliezer Kaplan, came back from a visit to the United States with a pessimistic assessment of the amounts that could be raised for the impending war effort. His estimate was that five to seven million dollars at

"I have had two great privileges in my life," *Golda has said. "One, that my name was included among the signatories of Israel's Proclamation of Independence. The second — my mission as Israel's* ▷ *Minister to Moscow." Golda is shown with Moshe Sharett, then Israeli Foreign Minister, prior to taking up her duties in the Soviet capital.*

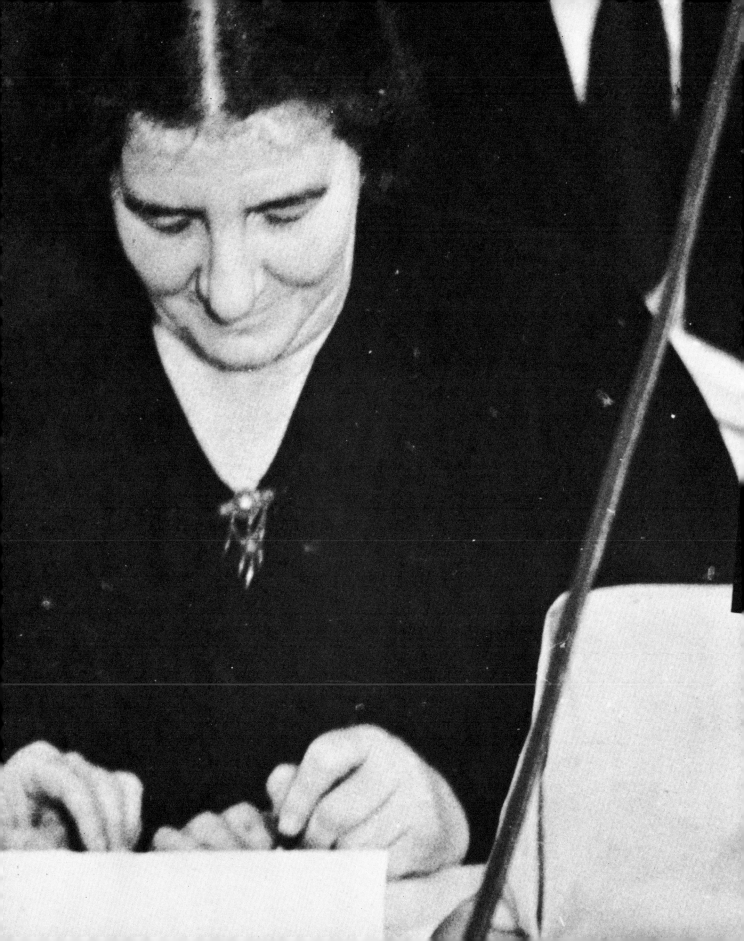

most could be raised among American Jews — a small fraction of what was needed.

At the Agency executive session which wrestled with this problem, Ben Gurion proposed that he and Kaplan go to the United States to arouse the Jewish community there to a greater degree of giving during those troubled days. As Ben Gurion voiced this proposal, Golda countered with a proposal of her own — she would go on this mission. She turned to Ben Gurion and said: "I cannot do what you are doing here, but whatever you'll be able to do in the United States, I can do, too." Ben Gurion refused to accept the offer and insisted that he should be the one to go. Golda asked for a vote, and the decision adopted by the executive was that she be sent.

Arriving in New York on January 19, 1948, she learned that, two days later, a convention of the Jewish Federations and Welfare Funds was to open in Chicago, to discuss the welfare needs of the Jewish people in the United States and abroad.

Golda's appearance before the convention delegates stirred the representatives of American Jewry as never before.

She described the struggle in which the Jewish community of Palestine was engaged — the dangers, the heroism, the sacrifices. "All that we are asking of world Jewry, and first and foremost from the Jews of the United States," she declared, "is that we be given the possibility to fight on. I didn't come here to save seven hundred thousand Jews. The Jewish people has lost six million in the war, and it would be sheer gall on our part to sound an alarm to save 700,000 now in danger. But — if these 700,000 are enabled to stay alive, then the Jewish people will survive and Jewish sovereignty will endure. And if these seven hundred thousand are annihilated, it will mean the end of the dream of the Jewish people for a Jewish homeland. We have the spirit, but this spirit alone cannot stand up to rifles and machine-guns ... the element of time is now of the utmost importance ... I have come here to tell you that within the next few weeks we will need between twenty-five and thirty million dollars, so that we will be able to do what we have to do.

"We are not a better group of people than others. Nor are we the best Jews among the Jewish people. But it happens that we are there and you are here. I am sure that if we were here and you were there, you would be doing what we are doing and would be asking us to do what you have to do."

"The decision as to whether or not we should fight is not up to you. We have already decided. You can determine only one thing: whether we or the Mufti will win this war."

Golda's words were spoken from the heart, extemporaneously, without notes. A wave of emotion swept the audience. Someone in the audience said: "We never saw anybody like her. So direct, so strong, so impressive — just like a woman out of the Bible..."

For two and a half months, Golda Meir traveled the length and breadth of the United States. She spoke at hundreds of meetings and gatherings, and amassed fifty million dollars — twice the sum that even the most imaginative had dared to dream of.

Immediately after May 14, 1948 — the day that the State of Israel was officially proclaimed — Golda was again sent hastily back to the United States. It was decided that the wave of enthusiasm that had swept American Jewry following the proclamation of Israel's sovereignty called for her to go again, and to transform the enthusiasm into the practical language of funds needed to acquire arms to defend the newborn State.

Now she appeared in the United States as the representative of the State of Israel. And in spite of the war being waged in 1948, the sacrifices and the gravity of the young nation's situation, Golda Meir would declare to beaming audiences: "Imagine! We have a country!"

MISSION
TO THE JEWS
OF SILENCE

An historic moment: Golda Meyerson, Israel's first Minister to Moscow, presents her credentials to a Vice-President of the U.S.S.R.

But now her stay in America was very brief. Toward the end of May, Golda received a cable from the new Foreign Minister of Israel, Moshe Sharett, asking her to accept an appointment as Israeli Minister to the Soviet Union. Golda did much soul-searching. "After all," she confided, "we do have a State now, I want to be home, not thousands of miles away from it." But pressure was brought to bear on her from all sides, and she finally agreed to accept the post. She had to be back in Israel at the beginning of June and make preparations to leave for Moscow.

Golda, accompanied by a retinue of twenty-one staff members of the Israel Legation posted to the Soviet capital, arrived in Moscow on September 3, 1948.

Golda served in Moscow for seven months. She has never forgotten the Jews of the Soviet Union. On one occasion she said : 'In my years of service I have been exceptionally privileged twice : to have my name and signature on the Declaration of Independence of the Jewish people, and my diplomatic mission as Israeli Minister in Moscow.'

A few days after Golda arrived in the Russian capital, the Yiddish periodical *Einikeit* published a sharp anti-Zionist article, written by the Soviet Jewish writer, Ilya Ehrenburg. This article heralded the cooling off in relations between the Soviet Union and the State of Israel, which began shortly after Golda's arrival. Those were the warning signals.

During Golda's stay in Moscow, mass demon-

On a less formal occasion, Mrs. Meir is shown with Russian officials following presentation of her credentials. At right, Soviet Ambassador Zorin, currently stationed in Paris.

The place, Moscow. The time, Rosh Hashanah, 1948. The photograph was taken near the Moscow Synagogue when thousands of Soviet Jews came to gaze in wonder at an Ambassador of the State of Israel to the Soviet Union. The crowd was estimated at 40,000 people, compared to the average 2,000 worshippers in the High Holy Days.

strations on behalf of Israel took place in the Russian capital. They were to be the last such outpourings, and Golda was deeply moved by them. Like many others, she had believed that after so many decades of Communist rule, nothing would be left within Soviet Jewry of a religious or national sentiment toward the Jewish people or the Land of Israel. It was clear that the Soviet regime itself had not assessed the situation correctly. Things took a sharp turn; in the ensuing months, one after another, all organs of Jewish culture were throttled — newspapers, theatres, institutions.

When Golda attended the Great Synagogue in the Russian capital on the first Sabbath following her arrival, tens of thousands of Jews besieged the building, just to catch a glimpse of her or touch her coat.

An eyewitness, Mordechai Henzin, reported: "The synagogue was packed; the atmosphere was electric. A huge banner across the wall proclaimed *Am Yisrael Hai* (the Jewish people lives). Someone shouted: 'She's coming!' The Jews rushed outside, I among them. I saw a tall woman with burning eyes, simple, modest, a daughter of the Jews of old, of the Bible, Golda. They all

Golda returns to Lydda Airport from Moscow. She is welcomed by Foreign Minister Sharett, right.

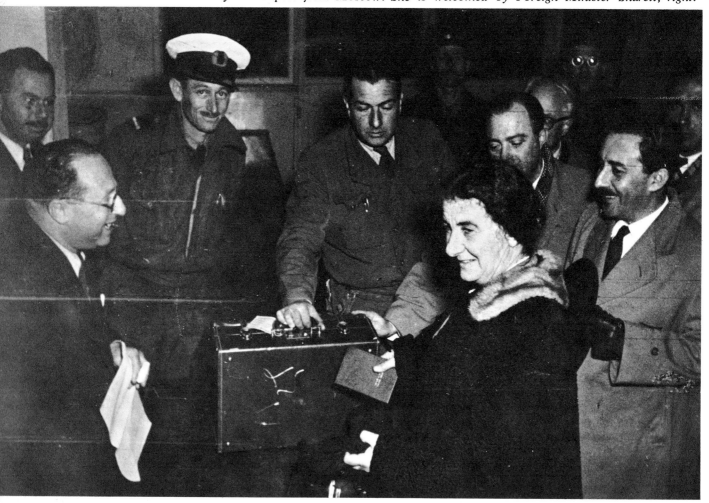

closed about her — persecuted, homeless Jews surrounded Golda. She was overwhelmed, and her tears were scarcely controllable. Their tears were all too easily seen as they touched her coat. She walked slowly through the pressing throng. Golda! Golda! Golda! rose the cries around her."

Another impressive recollection from those days is a meeting with the wife of the Russian Foreign Minister of that time, Vyacheslav Molotov. Mrs. Molotov approached Golda at a reception held in the Molotov home in November in commemoration of the Bolshevik revolution, took her aside and began talking to her, in Yiddish. In reply to Golda's look of amazement, Mrs. Molotov explained: "I am a Jewess." She listened intently as Golda unfolded the story of Israel's development, agriculture, defense problems. Mrs. Molotov also talked with Golda's daughter, Sarah, and Yael, daughter of Legation Secretary Mordechai Namir; Mrs. Molotov simply could not tear herself away from the *sabra* girls. As she took leave of Golda, she said, tearfully, in Yiddish: "Would that everything go well with you. If it does, so will it for Jews all over the world."

The then Soviet Chairman, Kruschev, meeting Golda Meir in New York in 1960 managed to exchange a civil greeting, despite Russia's open anti-Israel bias.

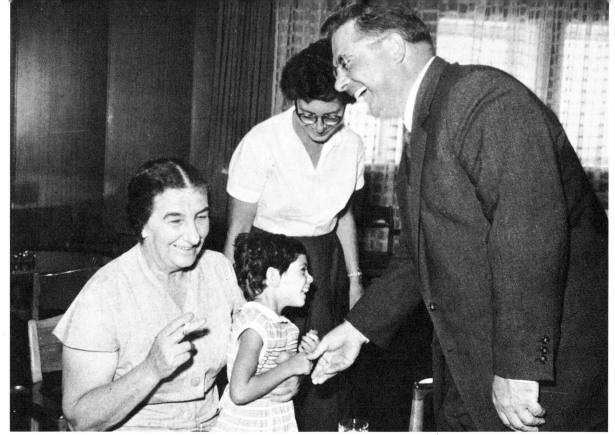

Russia's Ambassador to Israel in 1957, was amused by Golda's grandchild, with Golda's daughter.

A decade later, the Russian Ambassador to Israel and Mrs. Meir toasting peace!

THE MOST
BEAUTIFUL
YEARS

It was a foregone conclusion that Golda's presence in Moscow would be short-lived. She left Moscow on April 20, 1949 (her daughter and son-in-law remained there another eight months). But in Israel there were important tasks awaiting her. Following the elections to the first Knesset, as the first Cabinet was being put together, Golda was invited by Ben Gurion to join it as Minister of Labor.

Golda had this to say about the invitation many years later: "When I returned to Israel from Moscow, Ben Gurion offered me the post of

Golda's official photo, when she assumed office as Minister of Labor.

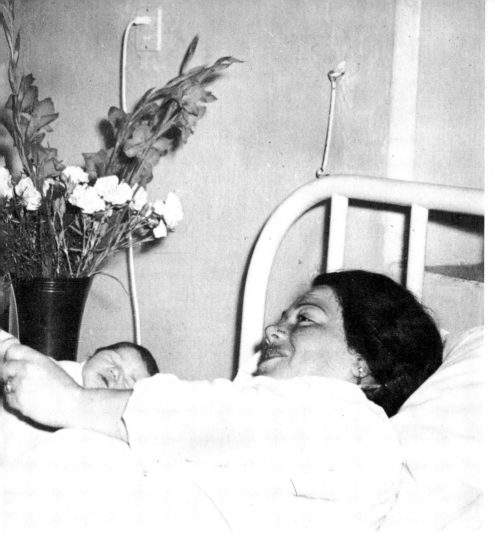

A young mother received from Golda the first National insurance grant for giving birth in Hadassah Hospital in Jerusalem.

Deputy Prime Minister in charge of development. I said : 'Not this ; I don't know a thing about development, and I don't want to be Deputy Prime Minister. If you want me in the Government — I want to be Minister of Labor.'"

Golda served as Minister of Labor for seven years — the happiest period in her life, she said later. That was what she liked — real work : constructive work, social work.

Golda came to this post with a significant background of experience garnered in the course of many years in the Histadrut executive. In the seven years of her Ministry there was a great upswing in housing enterprises, road networks spread throughout the country, and welfare legis-

lation was enacted to take care of the citizen from his first breath to his last. These were the years of mass *aliyah,* as hundreds of thousands of immigrants poured into Israel every year. Transit camps were put up all over the country, and Golda's foremost concern was to create employment for the newcomers and move them from temporary shacks to permanent homes. Despite incredible hardships and obstacles, the years of Golda's tenure were marked with complete success, as even her opponents readily admit.

Those were also the years when Golda's children were making a significant contribution to her happiness. Golda always was — and still is — the typical doting Jewish grandmother.

51

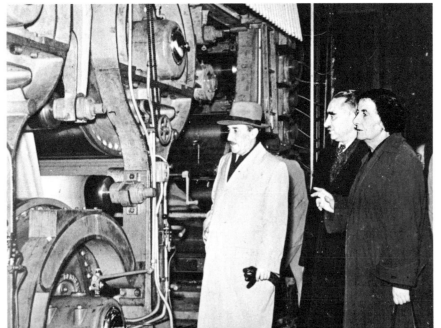

While Minister of Labor, Golda Meir established a rare relationship with workers and management in all spheres of Israel's economic life. Here she is seen on an official visit to the great enterprise of the American Paper Mills in Hadera.

As Minister of Labor, Golda went out into the country to see for herself how her Ministry's programs were developing. Planting a tree, laying a new plant's cornerstone, inspecting finished products, were all part of the job which she loved.

With Ben Gurion and Sharett, at a reception honoring the American Jewish leader, Jacob Blaustein.

As Minister of Labor, at a meeting in Geneva.

In the Knesset dining room: Golda and David Remez exchange a brief word with the Police Commandant.

With Premier Eshkol, during a mission to London.

At Haifa port, accompanied by Ada Maimon, greeting new immigrants to Israel.

At a reception in her honor.

In a familiar setting.

In Tel Aviv — a very informal Minister.

A VOICE
AMONG
THE NATIONS

Golda and Ben Gurion, in 1956, with the then chief of the U.N. observers, General Burns.

The growing schism between Ben Gurion and Foreign Minister Sharett came to a head in 1956; the moderate Sharett resigned and was replaced by Golda Meir (it was at this point that Ben Gurion insisted that she Hebraize the name Meyerson). The ensuing ten years of her service in this post were marked with grave crises, and Golda helped Israel weather them with her dignified and capable representation of the State on the international scene. Some people called her "Israel's most sentimental delegate to the world." It was generally agreed, among the international agencies with whom she came in contact, that never did Israel have a representative who engendered so much trust and sincerity. Her appearance on the international stage gave the impression — as it still does — that this woman bore on her shoulders the two thousand years of Jewish dispersion and was suffused with the burning faith in the justice of her cause. This sensitivity

achieved its peak when she addressed the United Nations after the Sinai campaign in 1956 and once again after Eichmann's abduction from Argentina.

And yet, it would seem that, in her decade of service as Foreign Minister, Golda did not engage in formulating political doctrine. Golda Meir's method was founded on a direct and simple style accompanied by a deep and warm faith which convinced friend and foe alike that here is a woman who believes in her cause and would fight for it. She never excelled in turning a phrase into a scintillating utterance. Her credo is the unsophisticated criterion: "Is it good or bad for Jews?"

Golda's assumption of her new post coincided with the events that reflected her activist approach — the eve of the Sinai campaign. The murderous acts of the Fedayeen infiltrators, dispatched by the Arab countries, primarily Egypt, were increasing. The Russians were pouring into Egypt modern arms and military equipment. It was clear that Nasser was preparing for a "second round," designed to wipe Israel off the map.

Few in Israel were aware of the preparations that were being made for the Sinai campaign. Golda was one of the few who did know. On October 29, 1956, Israeli forces broke through into Sinai, and in one week took control of the peninsula and the Gaza Strip.

The Sinai campaign, as well as the British and French assault on the region to regain control of the Suez Canal, nationalized a few months earlier by Nasser, aroused a tumult of criticism around the world. On November 1st, an emergency session of the United Nations General Assembly arranged a cease-fire. Tremendous pressure was put on Israel to withdraw from the territories it had taken in the fighting.

Golda headed the Israeli delegation to the United Nations. This was not her first appearance there ; three years earlier, as Labor Minister, she had presented Israel's case in the General Assembly against the persecution of Jews and the infamous doctors' trials in the Soviet Union.

The situation following the Sinai campaign was quite different. While in 1953 Israel's stand against Stalin's reign of terror gained universal sympathy, Israel was now labeled an aggressor; she had forfeited favorable public opinion for the sake of security. An Israeli delegation headed by Golda went forth to the world's forum to try to explain Israel's position to the world.

In her address at the United Nations, Golda

Germany's first Ambassador to Israel, Dr. Rolf Pauls, greets Golda when presenting his credentials to President Shazar, at right.

described the underlying causes of the Sinai campaign against the background of the continuous aggression on the part of Egypt. "The Arab states were arbitrarily granted the right to make war; Israel was arbitrarily given the responsibility for keeping the peace," she declared.

"But warfare is not a one-way street," she continued. "Is it surprising that a nation living under such conditions should try to save its life from the threat of continued attack against it from all sides?" she asked. She described the acts of murder committed against peaceful Israeli civilians, then said: "We are a small people, in a small and desolate land. We have made it come alive through our love and the labor of our hands. Strong forces are working against us. The disparity in strength is tremendous, but we have no choice but to defend our lives, our freedom and our right of security. We want peace, but we cannot wait for peace to come while we are expected to tolerate plots to destroy us. If the forces of our enemies are arrayed against us, they cannot demand of us that we provide them with the ideal condition for the execution of their intentions."

Golda's presence at the General Assembly and her many meetings with the representatives of various countries contributed a great deal to gradual improvement in the atmosphere at the world body.

After prolonged negotiations, in which the chief participants were America's Secretary of State John Foster Dulles, Israel's Foreign Minister Golda Meir, and Israel's Ambassador to the United States, Abba Eban, a compromise statement on Israel's withdrawal was hammered out.

On March 1, 1957 Golda announced Israel's withdrawal from the Sinai and Gaza territories, based on the following assumptions: free and innocent passage of Israeli shipping through the Straits of Tiran would be guaranteed by the United Nations and Egyptian forces would not be allowed to re-occupy the Gaza Strip.

Ten years later, the insincerity of the United Nations guarantees was revealed, when Nasser concentrated his troops in Sinai and blockaded the Straits.

This experience in 1957 left its mark on Golda. Following the Six Day War in 1967, she took a consistently tough stand against withdrawing from the cease-fire lines before an ironclad peace agreement had been achieved.

This is how she puts it: "Inasmuch as the argument between us and the Arabs does not concern the territory in which we should live, but whether we should live at all, then, so long as we do not get to talk with the Arabs on the basis of their recognition of our national existence, we on our part see no purpose served by going into the details of any arrangement."

One of the most difficult tasks entrusted to Golda in those years was to argue the justice of Israel's right to try Adolf Eichmann, following his abduction and clandestine trip to Israel. In June of 1960 Argentina lodged a complaint with the Security Council, accusing Israel of infringement of Argentina's sovereignty. Golda stood before the Security Council, in a speech which moved its listeners and dented world public opinion. She reviewed Eichmann's role in the annihilation of six million Jews in Europe: "Is this a subject for discussion in the Security Council?" she asked. "The Council is a body which deals with threats to peace. Will Eichmann's trial by the people to whose destruction he had dedicated all his energies constitute a threat to peace, even if the method of his apprehension in some way contravened Argentinian laws? Or didn't the threat to peace lie in the fact that Eichmann enjoyed freedom, Eichmann was not punished for his crimes, Eichmann was free to disseminate the position of his warped soul among the young generation?"

The diplomatic crisis was dispelled when Argentina accepted Israel's apology. Eichmann was placed on trial in Israel. The process took many months and resurrected the memories of the Holocaust, sixteen years after the end of the second World War, when it seemed that the memory of that horrible era was about to sink into oblivion.

Golda's term as Foreign Minister was also marked by the strong bonds of friendship formed between Israel and the new states that emerged in Asia and Africa.

Israel at the time embarked on a policy of extending assistance to developing countries — most of them had gained sovereignty during the preceding decade and a half — with manpower, technical and administrative guidance and in many other ways.

Golda regarded this program as being of prime humanitarian importance — to guide and help build new societies founded on social justice and to raise the living standards of the masses of people. This assistance transcended all political considerations, rooted as it was in the moral values expounded in the Bible. On many occasions Golda stressed that as long as there would be one starving child in Asia or Africa, Israel would regard itself duty-bound to help remove this blight.

No wonder, then, that Golda's visits in various African and Asian countries were received with enthusiasm and admiration.

Her first trip to Africa, early in 1958, was to Liberia, Ghana, Nigeria and the Ivory Coast, which was still a French colony on the eve of its independence. In Liberia, Golda was crowned head of the Gola tribe ; the event gave rise to a *bon mot* — that Golda had been crowned in Liberia as *Rosh Ha-Gola,* which is Hebrew for the leader of all Jews outside of Israel.

In the talks that the heads of the young African states had with Golda, they repeatedly stressed their request that as many Israeli advisors as possible be sent to guide their development, particularly in agriculture. Golda, in turn, would explain to them that the solution to their problems lay not in counselors but in training the young Africans themselves to become technicians, agronomists, farmers and experts of all kinds.

"Send your people to our *kibbutzim* and *moshavim* for a period of six months or a year," she told them. "When they return they will be accom-

panied, if necessary, by experts from Israel. But in the meantime they themselves will learn how to set up and manage farm cooperatives."

Her second visit to the African continent was in 1960. The interim years had strengthened the links of friendship and deepened the feeling of trust between African states and Israel. Many of Africa's heads of state took advantage of this visit to voice their gratitude to Israel and its Foreign Minister. Golda was even exhorted at one point to change the name of her Ministry to the "Ministry of Friendship."

Former French Foreign Minister Christian Pinaud, at a luncheon in Paris honoring Golda, during the height of Franco-Israel amity.

As Foreign Minister of Israel, Golda had to travel extensively. Top right, in London, in 1958, she is shown with then Foreign Secretary Selwyn Lloyd: below, in Paris, with Couve de Merville, and above, with Pierre Mendes-France—in Brussels, time out for a brief smoke.

A diplomatic laugh — Golda with Danish Labor Minister ▷ Perh Hekrop.

At the airport to welcome Golda upon her arrival in Amsterdam is Prime Minister Luns of the Netherlands.

Skimming over Amsterdam's harbor in a launch, Golda waves "Shalom" to the Israel freighter "Tel Aviv".

With Prime Minister and Mrs. Hans Otto Kerag of Denmark, during Golda's visit to Copenhagen in 1961.

In Italy, with Prime Minister Fanfani.

In Iceland, visiting the site of the first Parliament in the Western world, at Tingolier.

Listening with sympathy to the problems of an Icelandic laborer.

In Stockholm, Golda goes backstage to thank young actors after a children's theatre performance in her honor.

Outside No. 10 Downing Street, with Sir Alec Douglas-Hume.

In London, with Foreign Secretary Michael Stewart.

Responding to a palace guard's salute, on her way to visit Sweden's King Gustav.

69

Outside Averell Harriman's residence in New York, during the height
of the hula hoop craze.

On an official visit to Chile, flanked by a color guard.

*With President Kennedy at the White House;
lunching in New York in 1958 with the then
Senator Kennedy.*

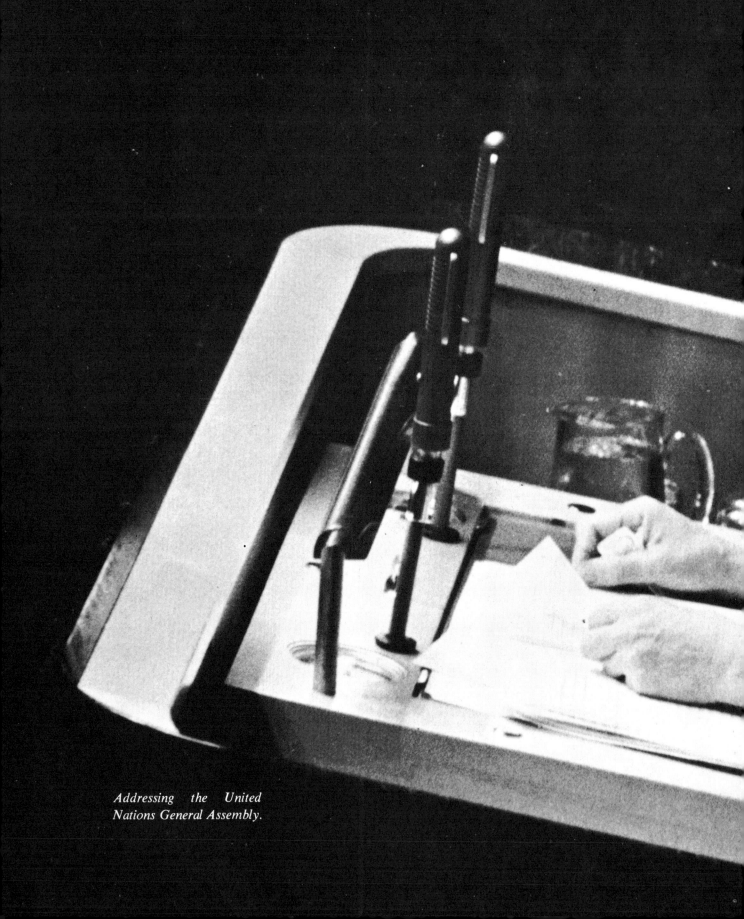

Addressing the United Nations General Assembly.

Arriving in New York in 1957 as Israeli Foreign Minister.

A friendly exchange with Dr. Ralph Bunche.

Dag Hammersjold, then Secretary General of the United Nations, stops at Mrs. Meir's desk.

Conferring with members of the Israel delegation at the U.N. in 1957, shortly after the Sinai Campaign.

An informal meeting in New York with Israeli journalists. Michael Comay, then Israel's Ambassador to the U.N. looks on (extreme right)

In a rare moment of doodling.

Golda Meir and Abba Eban, at a U.N. session.

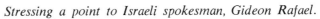

Stressing a point to Israeli spokesman, Gideon Rafael.

A deft touch, and the hairdo is fine again.

Receiving a confidential message in one of the United Nations' lounges.

Attention is riveted to speakers addressing the July 1957 meeting of the U.N. Assembly.

One unidentified speaker makes her smile.

In Liberia, with Israeli diplomat Ehud Avriel. ▷

81

In Lagos, dancing with the Nigerian Foreign Minister.

◁ *A friendly handshake with a leading Nigerian chieftain.*

Ghana's Minister of Public Works invites Golda to his nation's Independence Day celebrations.

Learning how to carry burdens on her head.

Dancing Israel's famous Hora folk dance with Mrs. Kenyatta and students in Kenya.

With President Jomo Kenyatta and Tom M'Boya, in Kenya.

At a celebration where she was presented with a tribal chief's footstool. With President Tubman of Liberia, right.

Joining in the local ceremonies.

In Monrovia, where she was designated a "Paramount Chief."

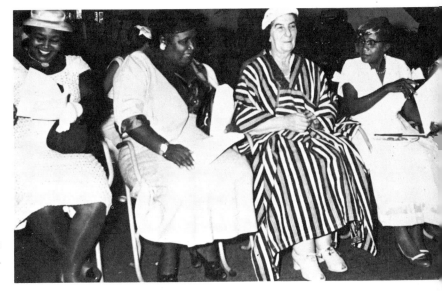

Golda was inducted into a village clan in a Liberian village. Ceremony included holding a hen and bowlful of eggs.

As guest of honor at a reception given in her honor in the Philippines.

Visiting a home for underprivileged children near Manila.

IN EVERY GOVERNMENT

Between 1949 and 1965, Golda served in every Cabinet of the Israel Government — for seven years, as Minister of Labor, and for nine as Minister of Foreign Affairs. At right, she is shown seated at Ben Gurion's side, during a Cabinet meeting.

In 1959, the Cabinet members proceed to the residence of the President.

Golda as a member of Ben Gurion's Cabinet of 1955.

The Cabinet in 1952.

The Cabinet in 1954.

959, Golda Meir, as Foreign Minister.

June 1963, with Eshkol, the new Prime Minister.

Israel's fourth Prime Minister, presides over the first Cabinet session of the new Israel Government.

AMONGST
FRIENDS

December 1967 : as one of Israel's leading socialist leaders, Golda Meir attended an international meeting in England. She is pictured with former French Foreign Minister Guy Mollet and George Brown, on her left, then British Foreign Secretary.

Camil Hausmans, veteran Belgian socialist leader, visited Israel in 1960 and participated in Israel's annual Independence Day celebration.

In 1967, Golda met with Willy Brandt, then Foreign Minister of West Germany, and today Chancellor.

At a worldwide socialist gathering, Mrs. Meir greeted Italy's Deputy Premier, Pietro Nenni.

With James Roosevelt, left, FDR's eldest son, and, below, with Eleanor Roosevelt. The late Mrs. Roosevelt and Mrs. Meir were close friends for many years.

With American labor leaders George Meany, right, and Walter Reuther, Golda is shown at a dinner meeting in the U.S.

With an old friend and supporter, David Dubinsky.

Arthur Goldberg, former U.S. Supreme Court Justice and American Ambassador to the United Nations, was greeted warmly by Mrs. Meir upon his arrival in Israel in 1968.

102

AMONG THE PEOPLE

Diplomat and leader of her people, Golda Meir
is also a typical Jewish grandmother, as shown in
this candid photograph. She is taking her grandchild for an early morning stroll.

Visiting her daughter and son-in-law and grandson, Saul, in K i b b u t z Revivim in the Negev is always a source of joy for Golda.

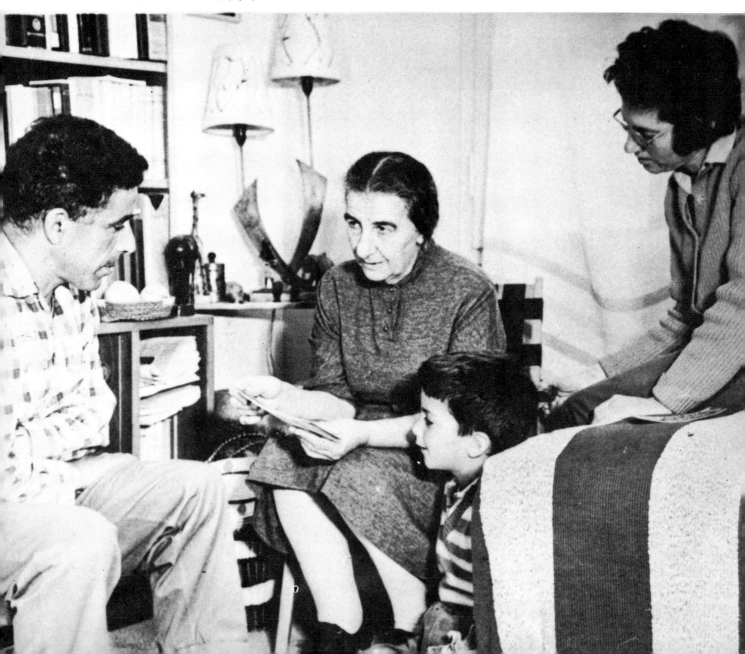

With son Menahem, daughter-in-law and two of their three children — precious moments of grand-motherly pleasure.

Three sisters, one of them a Prime Minister.

With the younger generation in the Revivim kibbutz dining room.

Between cares of state, Golda manages to find time to be with her sisters in the United States and members of their families.

When a grandson is entered into the Covenant of Abraham, at a Bris ceremony, it is a moment for rejoicing.

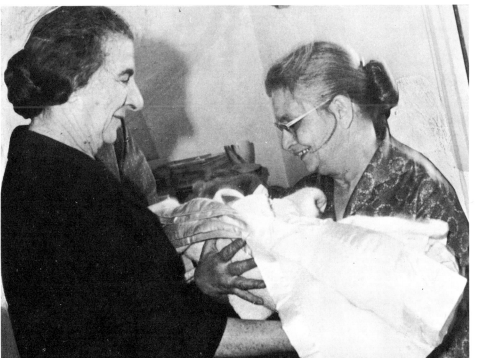

An anonymous soldier embraced Golda near the Western Wall, at the end of the Six Day War.

Visiting an Israel Army Camp in 1949.

On an official visit to an Israeli submarine.

Visiting Chen officers (Israel's Women's Corps).

As an ordinary participant in an early Israel Independence Day celebration, held at the Ramat Gan Stadium.

During the Eichmann trial in Jerusalem, the camera caught Golda Meir brushing away a tear.

◁ After leaving her post as Foreign Minister, she no longer had a car and driver, and could be seen queuing up for a bus like any Israeli citizen.

Golda made her points emphatically. Facing her is Zalman Shazar, President of Israel.

With Ze'ev Sharef, Minister of Finance.

With Mapai leader Reuven Barkat

With two Israeli diplomats, Ehud Avriel, right, and Haim Balzan,
she enjoys a light moment.

With Nechama Lif-shitz, the Jewish songstress from Soviet Russia, following her emotional premiere performance in Tel Aviv.

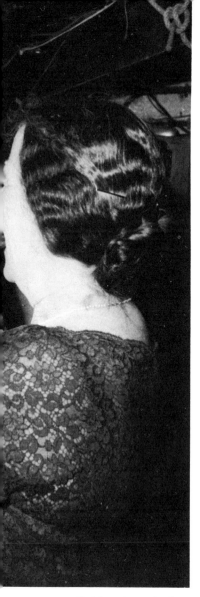

With her lifelong friend, Hannah Rovina, one of Israel's leading actresses — backstage with the actress, after a premiere performance.

With Pablo Casals, an old friend of Israel and her son's mentor.

Arab women living in the Galilee presented Mrs. Meir with a sample of delicate embroidery.

With leaders of Israel's Druse community. One of them is a member of the Knesset.

Participating in a Bedouin ceremony, Mrs. Meir extends the good wishes of the Israel Government.

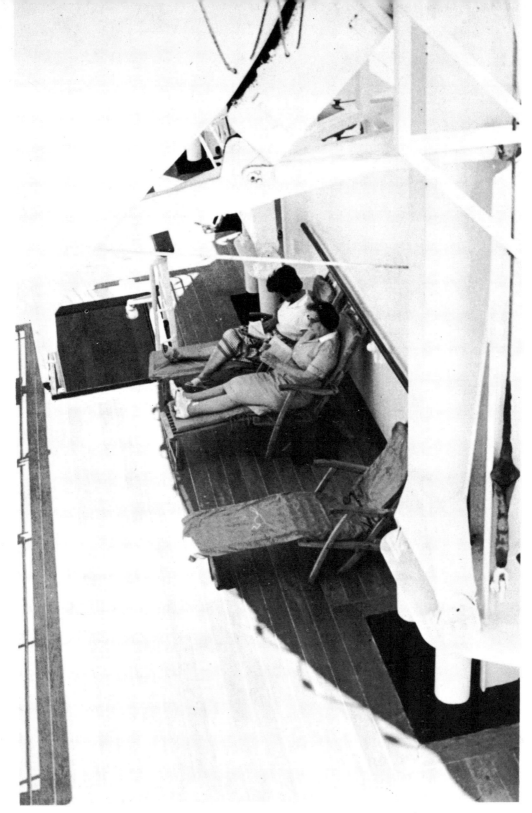

Time out for a brief rest aboard an Israeli liner cruising in the Mediterranean.

THE GOAL
OF UNITY

The issue of Israeli-German relations was one of the reefs on which the Golda-Ben Gurion craft struck, after decades of smooth sailing. Ben Gurion was at first inclined to go along with her more stringent stand in the matter, as she expressed it in the Knesset debate in 1963 about the activities of the German scientists in Cairo. One of Ben Gurion's close colleagues, however, considered Golda's intransigence sufficiently serious and urgent to warrant a journey to the Galei Kinneret Hotel in Tiberias, where Ben Gurion was vacationing. Ben Gurion was persuaded that the tough line taken by the Foreign Minister and intelligence chief Issar Harel was not justified and was based on an exaggerated evaluation of the importance of the scientists working in Egypt.

The underlying cause of the friction between Golda Meir and Ben Gurion was the reaction to frequent interference in the work of the Foreign Ministry by Defense Ministry people — young men whom Ben Gurion was drawing to his side, much to Golda's displeasure. As the Defence Ministry staff kept by-passing the Foreign Ministry, Golda made up her mind that this encroachment was untenable and intolerable; inevitable clashes followed, terminating with Golda's resignation, which she withdrew only after much pleading by Ben Gurion and his promise to put a stop to the situation.

When the rift between Ben Gurion and the late Levi Eshkol occured, early in 1965, Golda placed herself unequivocally at Eshkol's side. She opposed Ben Gurion's demand that one old political issue in particular should be resurrected; she was also in favor of strengthening the labor front through party mergers.

For precisely the latter reason, Golda opposed the splinter party founded by Ben Gurion and came out forcefully against it in the elections for the Knesset, held later that year. The Labor Party won handily and the splinter group fell far below expectations. Precisely at this juncture, Golda informed Eshkol that the time had come for her to retire and that she would not serve further

122

With Ben Gurion, just before May 15, 1948.

With Ben Gurion in London, in 1961.

Through their long years of working together, Ben Gurion always maintained the highest regard for Golda Meir.

as a member of the Government. Among her reasons, she cited the long and arduous years of public service she had given, as well as her desire to catch up on lost time with her family.

Still, Golda's hope for a slow-down in the pace of her public service and for time in which to devote more of herself to her family, personal matters, rest and reading did not materialize.

Golda Meir was the personification of the labor movement, regardless of the post that she happened to be filling at any given time. She was now the highest ideological authority in the party. Her colleagues pleaded that she accept the post of the party's secretary-general; they were convinced that in the light of imminent challenges facing the party — consolidation of the merger and the return of dissidents to the fold — only Golda was capable of conducting this important post. Golda debated the matter with herself for some time, then decided to accept the position for a limited term.

Golda elevated the secretary-generalship to an unprecedented level of importance and efficacy.

Golda took a staunch stand on vital matters in the months preceding the Six Day War. When it was mooted that in order to form a wall-to-wall coalition Eshkol should give up the Defense Ministry, Golda was adamant. "I never had any doubt that we will win the war. I had no doubt for a minute that there would be a war as soon as Nasser concentrated his army in Sinai and demanded the removal of the U.N. troops. I knew that our Defence Forces had been properly prepared, and therefore it was an injustice to Eshkol to maneuver him from Defense. At the same time, I was convinced that there was a need for national unity more than in the past. I agreed to the co-option of more ministers from other parties to the Government. I was convinced that in order to satisfy public opinion it would be advisable that Yigal Allon leave the Labor Ministry and assist Eshkol in his task as Defense Minister". She declined Eshkol's invitation to join

the national unity Government, but when Mapai ratified its formation, she nevertheless was loyal to the decision and assisted in its implementation.

At long last, on August 1, 1968, Golda completed her term of duty in the party. Her dream of a private life, of devoting herself to friends, of talking to young people and touring the settlements was about to come true. And it did — for six months, which she spent visiting *kibbutzim*, spending time with youth groups and, wherever she appeared in public, spreading the principles and ideas which had always guided her.

Her concepts of an ideal society were simple: we should know how to maintain the balance between vision and reality.

Golda has taken a firm stand on Israeli policy regarding the territories taken by the Israel Defense Forces in the Six Day War. She is unequivocally opposed to making detailed plans and drawing maps and boundary lines, so long as "there's no one to talk to." She says: "I do not go along with the principle of an unlimited Land of Israel, but I do not presume to ask any other Jew to give up an inch of the Land."

On another occasion she said: "I have set for myself a number of guide posts. First of all, what we should not give up under any circumstances — neither Jerusalem nor the Golan Heights nor Gaza nor Sharm a-Sheikh. Secondly, even if peace is attained, we will not be able to give up boundaries which provide us with a defensive position vis-a-vis our neighbors. I want borders which will give us the upper hand in case we are attacked. I want a Jewish state with a large Jewish majority. I like Yigal Allon's plan — a *cordon sanitaire* around the West Bank territory — because it doesn't take in the larger part of the Arab population." Then, in a typical afterthought: "It may be that the party should concern itself not with maps and physical borders but with ideological maps and borders."

During her term of office as secretary-general of the Labor party, and in the brief months before she became Prime Minister, Golda devoted a good deal of attention to strengthening Israel's bonds with world Jewry. Returning to Israel at the end of 1967, from a mission of several weeks to the United States, she aroused her party and public opinion in general to the need of approaching the challenge of *aliyah* — Jewish immigration to Israel — with far-reaching changes designed to stimulate *aliyah* and to provide proper tools for absorbing immigration.

She demanded that a supreme authority be set up for problems of immigration and absorption, to be operated jointly by the Israel Government and the Jewish Agency. She established in the Labor party a special commission for these matters. The party recommended that the two elements, immigration and absorption, be separate; the first would be handled, as previously, by the Jewish Agency, and the second by the Government, headed by a Minister. This recommendation, which was later accepted by the Israel Government and the World Zionist Organization, was not to Golda's liking. She was opposed to a schism between the two programs and remained firm in her conviction that a joint authority of the Agency and the Government would provide the best solution.

A world conference of Jewish organizations, to examine the reciprocal ties between the State of Israel and the world Jewish community was held in January of 1969, in Jerusalem, on the initiative of Prime Minister Levi Eshkol.

According to many among those present, Golda Meir's appearance at the summary sessions was one of the conference highlights. She dwelt at length on the dangers of assimilation among Jews in the free world and said: "Today in Israel we have a situation of no-war, no-peace, yet blood is spilt here every day. In Russia the distress of the Jews takes another form, but you, the Jewry of the free countries, are fighting the one great

Moshe Sharett receives a special accolade from Golda, following his talk at a Labor Party conference.

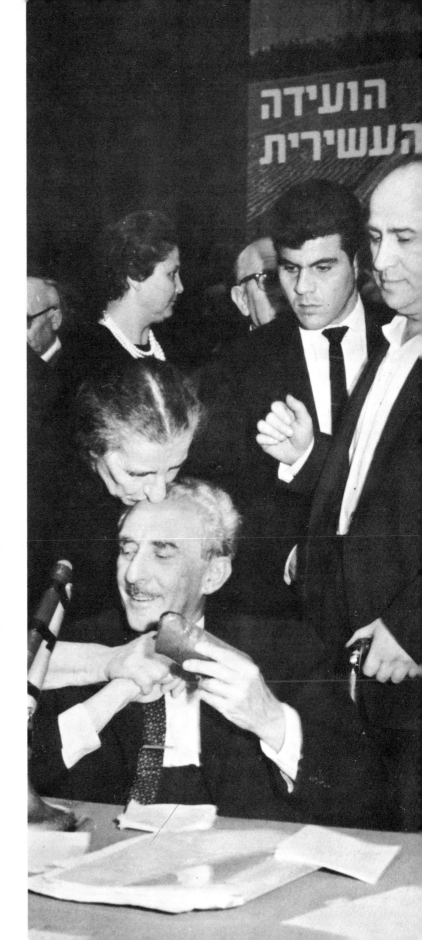

battle for the survival of the Jewish people. To tell you the truth, I don't know who is engaged in the heavier battle, we here in Israel or you. We repulse the attacks of our neighbors and we know what we are fighting for. They attack us with tanks and planes, and we defend ourselves with the same weapons. On the other hand, the struggle being waged by Jews all over the world is not a physical one, and I wonder whether all the Jewish communities have the necessary means to fight back. I have in mind specifically those Jewish communities in the world which are facing a grave danger — the danger of the disappearance of the Jewish people as a result of assimilation.

In the United States, I was told no Jew can say for sure that his grandson will be a Jew like he is. This is one of the most frightening things I have ever heard. What can the American Jew do? What can American Jewry do to make it possible for every one of its Jews to feel sure that his grandchild will also be a Jew?

"This is not a matter involving American Jewry only. It is of grave concern to the State of Israel as well."

From the need to share responsibility for the survival of Jewry, Golda went on to review the weeks preceding the outbreak of the June 1967 war, the war and its aftermath, and particularly the return for the worse that Israel's image took in world public opinion.

"What defect is there in Israel's image?" she

Visiting the Tel Aviv Hatikvah quarter, Golda finds a warm welcome.

During election campaigns, Golda could also be found talking at small private gatherings.

asked. "Can it be that, after all that we have undergone in Dachau and Auschwitz, the world still expects us to see Jewish blood shed and keep quiet about it, not to get excited but to act like wise and cool-headed people. We shall never keep quiet — never! There is no reason or purpose for Israel's existence if it is to make no move to protect every Jew everywhere."

In a call to Jewish youth from all over the world to come to Israel, Golda said: "We are not asking them to come here to fight. We want them to come and live here, to come and be in on the ground floor of the kind of world that they seek and hope for but cannot find elsewhere.

"We believe wholeheartedly that they and their friends in Israel can build on the foundations of faith in a progressive society and among people worthy of what has been done here. We are sure that we can help them build the kind of world they want too."

Golda ended her address with words that stirred the conference: "People coming here have been asking us about our situation and how long we

can hold out. For two thousand years the Jews have lived under a barrage of distress. If someone would have asked our forefathers: 'How long will you be able to hold out?' I don't know what their answer might have been. We can't give you an answer, but one thing can be said — as long as we live, our children and grandchildren, and your children and grandchildren — the State of Israel and Jewish life everywhere will be defended at all costs. I fully believe that not only the young generation but I, as well, will live to see the day when Israel will be free, independent, safe, developed and democratic, proud of having created the kind of society that the Jew should create, and living in peace with its neighbors and the entire world. I remember that at the peak of the terror of the Holocaust, someone asked me what kind of consolation could there be for six million dead? Only one, I say: we shall create in this country such moral values, such decency and human dignity that all the people who had hated and persecuted us down the centuries will come to us to learn the true meaning of human dignity and human decency."

127

Yigal Allon, notes the exact moment of decision.

With Levi Eshkol.

Historic leaders (l. to r.): Moshe Sharett, Eliezer Kaplan, Golda Meir and Joseph Shprinzak.

Demanding unfettered Jewish immigration to British-Mandated Palestine, at a Haifa meeting.

128

Speaking to the World Zionist Congress session in Jerusalem.

At meetings that led to unification of Israel's principal Labor Parties.

Labor leader Yitzhak Tabenkin and Golda Meir, ushering in a new era of labor and unity in Israel.

130

PRIME
MINISTER
OF ISRAEL

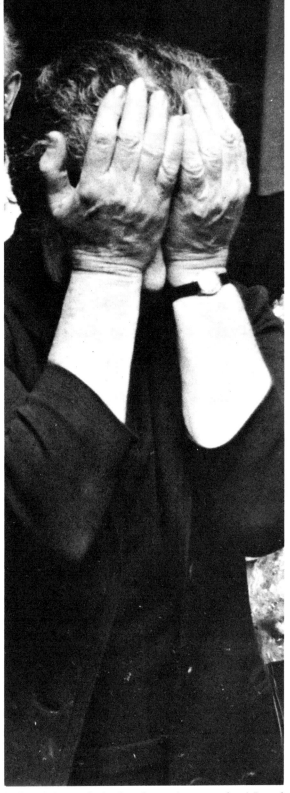

When informed she has been chosen to lead Israel as Prime Minister, Golda is overcome by emotion.

The passing of Prime Minister Levi Eshkol brought to the fore Golda's suitability to succeed him, despite the known fact that she wanted to limit her public activity and had even decided not to run for the next Knesset. Hers was the sole candidacy which met with no objection or controversy either in the ranks of the Labor party or among the other parties in the Government coalition.

The expression of confidence given to Golda by her own party and the other factions within the Government prevailed on her to accept the call of her country.

A member of the Labor party who attended the nomination session gave voice to people's sentiments: "I feel that Golda is hewn from the rock that this mission demands. She is endowed with the traits that this post demands. Her personality carries the required authority; her political experience is unusually rich; her standing among Jews of the world is incomparable; she enjoys respect in the international arena — in the West and among the Afro-Asian countries, from the days of her pioneering work in cementing relations between Israel and the awakening world; and she has it in her to engender the spirit of genuine coalition."

The session spent three hours listening to speeches in a similar vein, then put the motion to a vote. The tellers counted the results — none against. Pinhas Sapir, chairman of the session, banged his gavel on the table, announced the results and gave the floor to Golda Meir. The delegates moved forward in their seats. Golda would surely accept, they felt; the atmosphere in the Ohel Theatre building was charged with emotion.

Golda walked slowly to the platform, amidst total silence. Then, as she reached the rostrum, the hall broke out in thunderous applause. For a long moment Golda could not utter a word. When she finally began speaking her voice quivered a little, but soon it was steady and the breaks between the sentences gave way to her solid,

Tears overwhelm the stalwart woman leader when nominated to serve as Prime Minister.

Congratulations from everyday citizens, and a friendly word with veteran Israeli leader, Avraham Harzfeld.

133

The President of Israel, Zalman Shazar, formally charges Mrs. Meir with the task of leading the new Israel Government and signs the offical document of appointment.

homespun style. She told her fellow members of the party exactly what it meant for her and for them to assume responsibility for the welfare of the nation.

Golda spoke extemporaneously, without as much as a single written note in front of her, an unusual departure from the way that a candidate who is assured of nomination would prepare his acceptance speech. But this was Golda's way.

No matter how important the event — even in the question of unification of political parties — her talks are unrehearsed, unembellished by platitudes. This method, she believes, is the most direct line from the speaker's heart to the listener's.

In the approval of Golda's nomination by the other political segments of the country, a stumbling block appeared on the horizon due to ancient *halachic* law, of importance to the religious parties. Maimonides had ruled that "in Israel, all tasks are to be in charge of a man." Earlier in Golda's career, this bit of jurisprudence had deprived her of the support she needed to be elected mayor of Tel Aviv. This time the heads of the

religious parties found a legal loophole. They maintained that the situation now was not within the province of that law; they were not actually voting for Golda to be Prime Minister, but were extending a vote of confidence to the Government under her leadership.

The overriding significance of Golda's election was in the continuity which it gave to Israel's Government and public leadership. The anticipated struggle over who would be Levi Eshkol's successor did not materialize; the helm was turned over, in democratic and dignified fashion to a veteran leader of Israel.

On the very first day that Golda took over her new post, it was evident that an experienced hand was in control, despite the short notice that destiny had given her. Her colleagues immediately discovered that her familiarity with the workings of their Ministries would have done credit to a career diplomat.

At the same time, her manner of plain speaking and her direct approach to people and problems has not changed. She is still simple, folksy and to the point, whether her remarks are directed to the Knesset, foreign or local newsmen or foreign diplomats.

"She goes at it with all her might," remarked a senior Government official. "Golda Meir represents most of the nation, with good balance and exemplary consistency. She goes to all possible lengths to include the members of the Government in all the processes of consultation and decision. As far as bearing the burdens of her office is concerned, she shoulders them as if she were twenty years younger. Her capacity for work is amazing; the young ones in the Ministry have yet to catch up with it. The way she operates, all those puerile arguments about the leadership of the older generation having to make way for the younger generation are shown to be nonsense."

Certainly her energy, her courage and her determination to serve her country and her people at a time when they need her most, and have called on her most urgently, is an inspiration.

Elections to the Seventh Knesset were held seven months after Golda Meir became head of the Israel Government. Her popularity was at its peak. Wherever Golda appeared she was greeted with enthusiasm and affection. In a matter of months she was no more the leader of a party but a national figure, the symbolic image of Israel in a period of storms and stresses.

The extent of the general acceptance of her leadership was demonstrated in the election campaign. Golda Meir was the only one of all the leading personalities who did not come under attack from any of the contending parties. There was a unanimous opinion that Golda was the obvious and natural choice to head a Government, and the only person capable of maintaining a Government based on broad principles of common purpose and patriotic endeavour. Despite the political fragmentation so characteristic of Israel (16 parties vied for the 120 seats in the Knesset); despite the differences which arose within the Labor (alignment) Party ; despite the deep cleavages between the proponents of an unabridged Land of Israel and the advocates of yielding territory in return for a firm peace, and despite the noisy arguments between hawks and doves — the Labor Alignment, with Golda Meir at its head, won half the seats in the Knesset. The resultant victory at the polls, and the subsequent coalition Government, were largely a personal triumph for her.

What has been the secret of Golda Meir's suc-

The new Government of Israel. Mrs. Meir and Yigal Allon are seated alongside President Shazar.

cess as Prime Minister?

First, she was able to make short shrift of the threat to unity within her own party. At the beginning of her tenure it looked as though Moshe Dayan and former members of R a f i would secede from the Labor Party and form another party headed by Dayan. Her efforts prevented a split, and the Labor Party remained intact. In a remarkably short time, she had established herself as the national and party leader, in a unique role of first among equals, of Premier surrounded by colleagues. She has succeeded in establishing lines of communication to all the members of her Cabinet, the fiercest hawks as well as the most delicate doves. Her basic assumption has been that peace boundaries will have to be determined

The new Israel Government, with Mrs. Meir, as Prime Minister, and Yigal Allon, right, as Deputy Prime Minister, is toasted by President Shazar.

by the frontiers of Jewish demography, so as to assure the Jewish character of the State of Israel. "This is not the time for map making" she says, and draws on her considerable experience in foreign affairs to advise and negotiate. Her inimitable style can be detected in major Government statements. She has managed to simplify the involved expressions and to focus domestic and world attention on the formula of direct negotiations with the Arab countries.

Golda Meir was a major success as spokesman for Israel throughout the official twelve day visit to the United States, in late September and early October of 1969. In the course of this visit she met with President Richard M. Nixon and his advisers and toured the East and West Coasts where she also held meetings with the Jewish Communities. The talks with President Nixon centered on Israel's economic and military needs and on the ways of achieving peace in the region.

137

Mrs. Meir delivers her maiden address as Israel's Prime Minister.

The Cabinet is presented to the Knesset. A vote of confidence is asked for.

Knesset members give it overwhelmingly.

A Prime Minister without pretensions. At right, she visits the Revivim bomb shelter... a few precious minutes with her grandchildren... and even a little time out in the kitchen.

Visiting army encampments, bad weather notwithstanding, includes meetings with officers in the field like General Arik Sharon.

Her new personal bodyguard : Mordechai Rachamim, who foiled an Arab terrorist attack on an El Al plane in Zurich.

Viewing an ancient inscription on a newly-uncovered stone in Jerusalem.

Two of Israel's most popular leaders are pictured with Golda —Moshe Dayan and Yigal Allon.

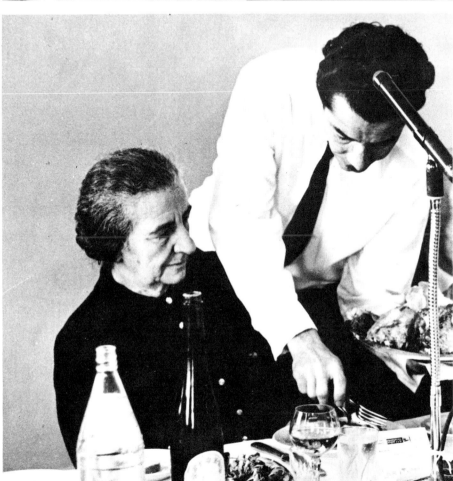

Formal dinners, speeches and waiters are back on Golda's daily routine.

143

Visiting liberated Jerusalem for the first time since she took office, Mrs. Meir receives a warm greeting. Mayor Teddy Kollek is shown with her ... at left, she unveils a plaque dedicating the Ramat Eshkol section in Givat Hamivtar, named for the late Israeli Premier ... below, touring the ancient areas of the hallowed city of Jerusalem.

Addressing the annual luncheon meeting of the Israel press corps.

The diplomatic corps extends greetings to Mrs. Meir.

Chatting with visiting American S

Israeli television has arrived and here Mrs. Meir is interviewed.

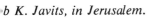

b K. Javits, in Jerusalem.

At a diplomatic reception, greeting Guatemala's envoy to Israel.

148

Independence Day 1969: a color guard presents arms as the Prime Minister proceeds to the residence of the President.

On a visit to London, the Israeli leader meets with British Prime Minister Harold Wilson.

A young winner at the Jerusalem Youth Bible Contest receives his prize from the Prime Minister.

At an open exchange with students of Bar-Ilan University.

An embroidered replica of the Druse structure is presented to the Israeli Premier.

In Jerusalem, Mrs. Meir meets with the leaders of Israel's minority communities, for a frank discussion of their problems.

Right: Joining with Druse leaders at a festive occasion ... Below: Golda removes her shoes upon entering what is purported to be the final resting place of Jethro, father-in-law of Moses, who is revered by the Druses.

151

Golda Meir has always had a reputation for being completely clear and unequivocal on questions dealing with Israel's foreign affairs and security. In her public speeches, and in diplomatic and party programs, she has always voiced complete confidence in the Israel Defense Forces' moral and military supremacy.

As Prime Minister she went out to see for herself Israel's most important post-Six Day War front — the Suez Canal. During one day she toured many advance positions in the Sinai, accompanied by Minister of Defense Dayan, Chief of Staff Bar-Lev, and other top Israeli leaders.

An informal honor guard, armed with Uzi submachine guns, meets with the Prime Minister.

En route to a forward position.

◁ The tour begins in a command car.

Luncheon guests of one of the advanced units.

Military details are reported to Mrs. Meir by Gen. Bar-Lev, center, while Gen. Gavish, right, and Minister of Finance Sharef, left, listen in.

Golda Meir's visit to the United States in early Fall, 1969 coincided with significant external and internal developments for Israel. She established an immediate and valuable rapport with the President of the United States, and is seen here in earnest discussion with him in the White House.

At the conclusion of the talks it emerged that the President of the United States understood the need for American military assistance to Israel. According to the American press, President Nixon was deeply impressed by Golda's personality and by her direct approach to the problems which the two of them had discussed. The President was reportedly insistent on the maintenance of the balance of power in the Middle East, while taking Israel's defense needs into consideration. He also recognized Israel's heavy economic burden caused by continuing defense demands, in addition to heavy commitments for social and educational

rehabilitation of thousands of immigrants from countries of dispersion and discrimination.

Golda's achievements were mirrored in her many appearances in newspaper headlines, and on radio and television, where she captivated her interviewers, the press, and the public with her straightforward and direct answers to provocative questions on Israel's policy.

At a National Press Club meeting Golda was asked :

Q : Did you get any 'gifts' for Israel during your current talks in Washington with U. S. officials ?

A : The talks have been "very pleasant and very friendly." There has not always been agreement in points of view but where there has been a disagreement it has been one among "very friendly" countries. U. S. Government policy has indicated a "sensitivity" to a balance of power in the Middle East. This policy is being followed now. I have reason to believe it will continue.

On the same occasion Golda was asked about her culinary prowess :

Q : Your grandson Gideon is reported to have said his grandmother is the best gefillte fish cook in all Israel. What is your recipe ?

A : As for my grandson, I'm afraid he's not objective about me just as – as his grandmother I'm not objective about him. As for the recipe, I note you have invited me back here — win or lose in the upcoming elections — to address your club again. I will do that and I'll arrange to come here a few days ahead of time so I can cook some fish for you. (laughter).

Her reply at the close of the "Meet the Press" TV program was very much like Golda :

Q : You have earned a reputation for being tough, but you don't seem very tough. How did you get that reputation, and does it worry you ?

A : Well, really that doesn't worry me, honestly, because all I do, I don't try to be tough and I don't try to be not tough. All I am trying to do to the best of my ability is to explain the desires and the aims of my people and my country.

In the course of her visit, Golda Meir met with many thousands of Jews, especially in the larger centers of Jewish concentration : New York, Philadelphia and Los Angeles. Everywhere she found understanding on the part of the State and Civil authorities and enthusiasm from the leaders and masses of the Jewish communities.

One of the more stirring occasions was Golda's visit to Milwaukee, where as a young girl of eight from Russia, she had received her American education in her formative years.

The most famous pupil of the public school on Milwaukee's Fourth Street met with the entire school of 1969 — and told the youngsters, all Negroes, that she had spent her most enjoyable years in their school, from the second grade through the eighth. The school principal presented Golda with a photograph of her class and said : "If you don't recognize yourself, here you are — the prettiest girl in the class." Golda shook her head and smiled, a smile which said "no need to exaggerate."

Her visit provided the teachers with an opportunity to teach the children about Israel. The school walls were covered with drawings of Golda Meir and newspaper photographs of her visits to the White House and the United Nations. Her appearance was greeted by the pupils with a lively rendering of "Hevenu Shalom Aleichem".

Israel's Prime Minister gave an emotional account of her first years in Milwaukee and spoke of the city with much warmth and affection.

"Here, for the first time, we had the feeling of freedom. The Czarist police used to attack the workers, and here I saw for the first time, police protecting the workers against any interference with their demonstrations on Labor Day. Here I acquired knowledge and made friends. Here I took the most important decision in my life — to settle in Israel and to share in the efforts of other workers to establish a sovereign Jewish state."

Golda Meir's visit to the United States came to an end with a farewell appearance at the U. S.

Labor Convention in Atlantic City. On this occasion she said to the cheering delegates :

"Israel seeks only a simple peace agreement signed by both parties. This is the only thing that has not yet been tried. This is what Israel wants."

The Prime Minister said Israel's efforts to negotiate a face-to-face peace agreement with her Arab neighbors is based on an effort "to plead only one thing — there must be equality between all peoples of the world for the right to live in freedom, in sovereignty and peace ... we want peace — real peace. This time it must be peace agreements between Israel and her neighbors, and agreed — on borders."

AFL-CIO President George Meany, who received a medalion of the city of Jerusalem from the Prime Minister, introduced her as the representative of a democratic country whose people "have been helping themselves in an atmosphere of hostility."

Members of the Israel Government have noted and favorably commented on the unique style which Golda has introduced into Cabinet sessions and into her work as Prime Minister. She comes to a Cabinet meeting with a clear agenda in her mind. She chairs Cabinet meetings in orderly fashion, approaching this task with the same personal touch which substituted flowers for the dictating machine and other office items which she first found on her desk : the less superfluous details, the better.

Golda Meir delegates many responsibilities and duties to her Ministers, which allows her to concentrate on matters of security and foreign relations.

Golda's daily schedule begins early in the morning with a perusal of the cables received overnight and an on-the-spot decision as to what matters she will handle personally. Then the meetings and appointments begin. Lunch is eaten during a session or an appointment, and the working day comes to an end late in the night.

People who know Golda claim that she finds it difficult to reconcile herself to the limitations

For her effectiveness in presenting Israel's case to the great American nation with unparalleled success, Golda relied on two fundamental characteristics, a frank approach and the human touch. This picture tells its own story, with President Nixon hugely enjoying a reply given by Golda Meir at a press conference in the White House.

imposed by her high office. She likes to do her own shopping, which understandably poses problems for her bodyguards. The very idea of bodyguards upsets and frustrates her, even though she understands that for the present, it cannot be otherwise. At times, however, she manages to elude them to go shopping or to relax with friends in a modest neighborhood restaurant.

To this day, when she returns to her home in Tel Aviv for the weekend, she cooks, bakes, and washes dishes — like any Israeli housewife.

When in Spring, 1969 she accepted the President's call to become Prime Minister after the passing of Levi Eshkol it was to avoid a confrontation between two opposing candidates for the post.

At that time, her tenure appeared to be limited to a transition period, until the elections.

By the close of that same year, and looking towards the 1970's and beyond, Golda Meir's political leadership of the State of Israel is secure, historically significant and uniquely inspiring.

In no time at all, Israeli troops were telling the Prime ▷
Minister about life along the Suez Canal front.

157

SBN 87631-020-X